THE TELL-IT-TOGETHER GOSPEL: MARK

THE TELL-IT-TOGETHER GOSPEL: MARK

Translated by Paula Gooder

Interactive storytelling tips by
Bob Hartman

First published in Great Britain in 2019

Society for Promoting Christian Knowledge
36 Causton Street
London SW1P 4ST
www.spck.org.uk

British Library Cataloguing-in-Publication Data
A catalogue record for this book is available from the British Library

ISBN 978-0-281-07922-3
eBook ISBN 978-0-281-07923-0

Typeset by Fakenham Prepress Solutions, Fakenham, Norfolk NR21 8NL
First printed in Great Britain by Ashford Colour Press
Subsequently digitally reprinted in Great Britain

eBook by Fakenham Prepress Solutions, Fakenham, Norfolk NR21 8NL

Produced on paper from sustainable forests

Contents

Introduction

The idea for this book emerged out of a conversation between Bob and Paula a few years ago. Bob wondered what it would be like to do his Bible storytelling with the actual text of the Bible, rather than a retold and cut-down version, but was unsure if any of the published translations would be quite right for what he had in mind. Paula had always wanted to try her hand at a modern translation of the text. So we decided to try something together. *The Tell-it-Together Gospel* is the result of this. You will find here a new translation of Mark's Gospel interwoven with suggestions for how to 'tell it together' using actions and audience participation. We hope that you will find it a fun way to tell the Bible story and to get as many people as possible, of all different ages, to join in.

A note on the translation . . .

The translation is a completely new translation of the Greek text by Paula Gooder. As far as possible, we have kept as close to the original as we can. At the same time, we were aiming for a lively, engaging translation that would make sense to as many people as possible, so we have used modern words and phrases in order to communicate some of the power of Mark's Gospel. But, at the same time, we have left in words that some people won't know, such as 'Pharisees' or 'Corban', because they are there in the original.

Staying faithful to the original while producing a readable text that sounds modern can be difficult to navigate, so sometimes it was necessary to add in a word or two to help the modern reader to make sense of the action. We tried to do this as little as possible, but occasionally we needed to explain who 'they' were in the text, as Jesus and his disciples (or someone else) had been introduced such a long time ago that the phrase didn't make sense as it stood.

. . . and a note on the actions

We have tried to spell out the actions as clearly as possible, in both the bold type we have used and in the instructions given. Being clear and confident is the best way to pass those instructions on to the members of your audience.

Tell them exactly what you want them to do and how you want them to do it. Model it for them, then do it with them, to give them confidence to do it too.

Read through the text and the actions ahead of time. Practise. The more familiar you are with the actions, the more confident everyone will be.

Do it with a smile on your face, unless the action calls for you to be serious or sad. Playfulness is key.

If another person is available, it can be really helpful for one of you to read the text and the other to lead the actions.

If there is some action you genuinely think won't work, feel free to leave it out or change it.

Above all, create a welcoming environment, where everyone is invited to join with you as you climb into the text and 'tell it together'!

Mark 1

How it all began

[1] The good news of Jesus Christ, the Son of God, began like this.

[2] Just like the prophet Isaiah had written a long time before:

'Look out! **(Have everyone shield their eyes with one hand, as if looking far in the distance.)** I am sending my messenger in front of you. He'll make a way for you.'

[3] A voice is shouting in the desert **(have everyone shout the next two lines after you)**: 'Make a way for the Lord. Make straight paths for him.'

(Now ask, 'So who do you think is the messenger? Who is making the path straight? Here he comes . . .')

[4] John, the one who baptized people, was in the desert. He was telling people about a baptism that turned their lives around so that all the wrong things they had done could be forgiven. **(Tell everyone to**

1

turn and face a different direction, shake their heads, as if they are shaking off water, and shout, 'I've changed direction! I'm forgiven. Hooray!') ⁵ Everyone came out from that area – from Judea and Jerusalem – and, as they admitted what they had done, John baptized them in the River Jordan. (**Tell everyone to turn and face a different direction, shake their heads, as if they are shaking off water, and shout, 'I've changed direction! I'm forgiven. Hooray!'**)

⁶ John's clothes were made from camel hair, which he tied with a leather belt, and he ate locusts (**everyone say, 'Icch!'**) and the honey (**everyone say, 'Mmmm'**) you can find in the wild. ⁷ He told the people: 'There's someone coming after me who is stronger than I am. I am not good enough even to bend down and take his sandals off. ⁸ I baptize you with water (**have everyone turn and face a different direction, shake their heads as if they are shaking off water, and shout, 'I've changed direction! I'm forgiven. Hooray!'**), but he will baptize you with the Holy Spirit.'

Jesus' arrival on the scene

⁹ At that time, Jesus came from Nazareth (which is in Galilee) and he was baptized by John in the Jordan. ¹⁰ As soon as he came up out of the water again (**have everyone shake their heads as if they are shaking off water and look up**), he saw the sky split apart and God's Spirit

2

coming down on him, looking like a dove. (**Have everyone make a cooing sound.**) [11] And a voice came out of heaven (**have everyone put their hand to their ear, as if they are listening**): 'You are my Son. I love you and am delighted with you.' (**Have everyone smile a broad smile.**)

[12] Right away, God's Spirit sent Jesus into the desert. (**Everyone looks worried and says, 'Oh, my!'**) [13] He was in the desert for 40 days being tested by Satan. (**Everyone looks more worried and says, 'Oh, dear!'**) There were wild animals with Jesus and the angels looked after him. (**Everyone gives a relieved sigh and says, 'Oh, good!'**)

Jesus began to tell people the good news!

[14] After John was arrested (**everyone whispers, 'Oh, no!'**), Jesus came into Galilee, telling people the good news of God (**everyone shouts, 'Oh, yes!'**) [15] and saying: 'God's kingdom is close. (**Everyone looks around.**) Turn your life around and believe in the good news.' (**Now everyone spins around.**)

[16] And he was walking by the sea of Galilee when he saw Simon and his brother Andrew; they were casting a net into the sea (because they were fishermen). (**Everyone casts a pretend net into the sea.**) [17] And Jesus said to them: 'Follow me (**everyone waves their hand in a 'follow me' fashion**) and I will show you how to fish for people.'

[18] They wasted no time, left their nets (**everyone throws their nets to the ground**) and followed him. (**Everyone walks in place after Jesus.**)

[19] Jesus went on a bit further and he saw James and his brother John, Zebedee's sons, in the boat mending nets. (**Everyone does a bit of pretend sewing.**) [20] Right away, he called them (**'follow me' hand motion again**) and they left their father with his employees (**everyone waves goodbye**) and followed Jesus. (**Everyone walks in place after Jesus.**)

Jesus healed a man . . .

[21] Jesus and the others went into Capernaum and right away, on the Sabbath, Jesus went into the synagogue and started teaching [22] and they were stunned by his teaching (**everyone shouts, 'Wow!'**) because he taught them as if he really knew what he was talking about – not like the experts in the law.

[23] At that moment, in the synagogue, there was a man with a troubled spirit and he shouted out loud (**tell everyone to shout the following lines after you**):[24] 'What have we got to do with you, Jesus from Nazareth? Have you come to destroy us? I know who you are! You are the Holy One of God!' [25] Jesus told him off and said (**everyone shouts the following line**), 'Shut up and come out

of him.' ²⁶ The troubling spirit shook the man from head to toe, shouted with a loud voice and came out of him.

²⁷ And everyone there was startled (**everyone shouts 'Wow!' again**), and started chatting among themselves: 'What is this? It's new teaching and it's powerful! Even troubled spirits do what he tells them.' ²⁸ The news about Jesus went out, right away, all round the whole area of Galilee. (**Everyone turns to a neighbour and says, 'Have you heard about Jesus? He's amazing!'**)

. . . and then lots more people

²⁹ And as soon as they came out of the synagogue, they went into Simon and Andrew's house, with James and John. ³⁰ And Simon's mother-in-law was lying down, ill with a really high temperature (**everyone slumps in their seat or leans back, hand on head, and says in a weak voice, 'I'm not feeling very well.' Stay in that position till your next line**), and right away they told Jesus about her. ³¹ And he came to her and helped her to get up, holding her hand, and the fever left her and she looked after them. (**Everyone sits up straight, smiles and says, 'I'm feeling much better now! Would anyone like a bite to eat?'**)

³² When evening came, after the sun had set, the people who lived near there brought to him all those who were ill or who

were tormented by demons. (**Everyone wraps their arms around themselves and whispers, 'I'm trapped.' Stay that way till your next line.**) ³³ And the whole city gathered around his door. ³⁴ And he healed many who were ill with all sorts of different illnesses and he got rid of many demons (**everyone unwraps their arms, lifts their hands in the air and cries out, 'I'm free!'**), but he wouldn't allow the demons to speak because they knew who he was. (**Everyone puts a finger to their lips and says, 'Shhhhh!'**)

He was so popular it began to be a nuisance

³⁵ He got up really early in the morning (**everyone stretches their arms and yawns**), while it was still night-time, and he went away to a place where no one else was and he prayed there. (**Everyone bows heads and folds hands in a praying motion.**) ³⁶ And Simon and the others with him hunted him down (**everyone looks round, as if searching for someone**) ³⁷ and they found him and said to him, 'Everyone's looking for you.' (**Everyone turns to a neighbour and repeats this line.**)

³⁸ And he said to them: 'Why don't we go somewhere else, to the towns near here? Then I can tell them the message of good news. That's why I came.' ³⁹ And he went through the whole of Galilee, telling the message of good news in their synagogues and getting rid of demons. (**Everyone lifts hands in the air and cries out, 'I'm free!'**)

⁴⁰ And a leper came to Jesus, begging him and grovelling before him, saying, 'If you want to, you could make me clean.' (**Everyone clasps hands in a pleading manner and repeats the leper's words to a neighbour.**) ⁴¹ Jesus felt for him deeply. He stretched out his hand and touched him and said, 'I do want to. Be clean.' (**Reach out your hand and touch your neighbour and repeat what Jesus said to the leper.**) ⁴² And right away the leprosy left him and his skin was smooth and healthy.

⁴³ Jesus talked to him sternly (**give your neighbour a stern look and point at him or her**) and sent him away, ⁴⁴ saying, 'Make sure that you don't tell anyone anything, but go and show yourself to the priest and take a sacrifice to the Temple to say thank you for your cleansing, as Moses said you should, so that everyone will know that you are well.' ⁴⁵ But the man went and began telling many people the news and spreading it about. (**Everyone turns to a neighbour and says, 'Have you heard about Jesus? He's amazing!'**)

This meant that Jesus wasn't able to go openly into any of the cities, so he stayed outside in the places where no one else was and, even then, the people came out to him from many different places.

Mark 2

A man was lowered through the roof

(You can divide your group into three for this one. Group 1 for the crowd in the house, Group 2 for the four friends, Group 3 for the experts in the law. Alternatively, if you like, you can simply have everyone do everything.)

¹ A few days later, when he came back again into Capernaum, the word went round that he was home. (**Have Group 1 whisper to their neighbour, 'Did you hear? Jesus is home!'**) ² And so many people came that there was no room, not even near the door (**have Group 1 budge up next to their neighbour**), and Jesus was telling them his message. ³ And some people came, bringing a man who couldn't walk, carried between four of them.

⁴ When they couldn't get to Jesus because of the crowd, they took the roof off the place where he was (**have Group 2 noisily pretend to bang on roof and tear off roof tiles and throw them over their shoulder**), and when they had dug out a hole (**now have Group

8

2 dig a hole), they let down the mattress the man was lying on. (**Finally, have Group 2 pretend to lower the man down.**) [5] And when Jesus saw the faith of the man's four friends (**have Group 2 smile and wave and shout, 'That's us!'**), he said to the man who couldn't walk, 'My child, whatever you've done wrong is forgiven.'

[6] And there were some experts in the law sitting there, and they thought to themselves (**have Group 3 repeat the following lines after you, in a grumbly fashion**): [7] 'Why is this man talking like that? He's speaking against God himself! Only God can forgive the things we've done wrong.' [8] Jesus knew right away what they were thinking to themselves and he said to them: 'Why are you thinking like this? [9] Is it easier to say to this man who can't walk, "Whatever you've done wrong is forgiven," or to say, "Get up, pick up your mattress and walk"?' (**Have Group 3 scratch their heads and mutter, 'Well, they're both quite hard, actually.'**) [10] But so that you might know that the Son of Man has the right to forgive the things people do wrong, he said to the man: [11] 'I say to you, get up, pick up your mattress and go home.'

[12] The man got up, and right away, in front of everyone, picked up his mattress and left. Everyone was astonished and worshipped God, saying (**have all three groups make an amazed 'Aaaaah' sound and then repeat the following line after you**): 'We've never seen anything like this before.'

Jesus mixed with the wrong kinds of people . . .

^{13} Jesus went out again by the seashore and a huge crowd came to him and he taught them. ^{14} And as he was walking along he saw Levi, Alphaeus' son, sitting in the tax office (**have everyone shout, 'Seaside Revenue, open today! Come and pay your taxes!'**) and Jesus said to him: 'Follow me,' and Levi got up and followed him. (**Have everyone stand up and walk in place.**)

^{15} Once, when Jesus was having dinner at his house – Jesus and his disciples were there as well as a lot of tax collectors and people who kept on doing the wrong things (**have everyone jump up and whoop and make noisy party sounds**) because a lot of them followed him – ^{16} the Pharisees saw him eating with tax collectors and people who kept on doing the wrong things (**repeat rowdy drunken action**) and said to his disciples: 'Why is he eating with tax collectors and other people who keep on doing the wrong things?' (**Repeat rowdy drunken action once more.**) ^{17} Jesus overheard what they said and answered: 'People who are strong and healthy don't need a doctor, only people who are ill. I didn't come to call people who know they always do the right things but those who know they're in the wrong.' (**Have everyone shout, 'That's us!'**)

. . . and didn't do what people thought he should

[18] John's disciples and the Pharisees were fasting (**have everyone say, 'We're not eating [make hungry tummy-rumbling sound]. We're praying, instead' [make praying hands]'**) so some people came to Jesus and asked him: 'Why do John's disciples and the Pharisees fast (**repeat previous words and actions**), but your disciples don't?' (**Have everyone say, 'We're still eating!' and make a gobbling-up motion and sound.**) [19] Jesus answered: 'Wedding guests don't fast while the bridegroom is still there. (**Repeat 'We're still eating!' and the gobbling-up motion and sound.**) For as long as the bridegroom is there, they can't fast. (**Repeat 'We're still eating!' and the gobbling-up motion and sound.**) [20] But the time is coming when the bridegroom will go away – they'll fast then. (**Have everyone say, 'We're not eating [make hungry tummy-rumbling sound]. We're praying, instead [make praying hands].'**) [21] No one sews a new patch of material (that hasn't been washed yet) on really old clothing; if you do, the new patch pulls away from the old cloth and the tear is worse than before. (**Have everyone hold up a piece of pretend cloth, shake their heads and moan, 'It's torn again!'**) [22] And no one puts new wine into leather bottles that have been used before; if you do, the wine will split the leather bottles, the wine will spill all over and the bottles will be ruined too. (**Have everyone look down at their laps and moan, 'It's spilled!'**) New wine needs to be put in new leather bottles.'

²³ Once Jesus was going through a field of ripe grain and his disciples were making their way too, picking the grains as they went. (**Have everyone pretend to pick up a bit of grain, pop it into their mouth and chew it.**) ²⁴ And the Pharisees said to him: 'Look! Why are they doing something they shouldn't do on the Sabbath?' (**Repeat previous action.**)

²⁵ Jesus said, 'Haven't you read what David did, when he and the people with him really needed food and were hungry? ²⁶ He went into God's house (Abiathar was high priest then) and he ate the special bread (**have everyone pretend to pick up a bit of bread, pop it into their mouth and eat it – pretty much the same action as before!**), which only the priests are allowed to eat, *and* he gave it to those who were with him.' (**Repeat the previous action.**) ²⁷ Then he said to them: 'The Sabbath was made for people; people weren't made for the Sabbath.'

Mark 3

Another healing and more trouble

(Divide your group into three. The group in the middle will play the man with the injured hand. The groups on either side of them will play the Pharisees and the Herodians.)

¹ Jesus went into the synagogue again and there was a man there whose hand had become stiff and curled up. (**Have the middle group hold out one hand in a stiff and curled-up position.**) ² They were keeping their eyes on Jesus to see if he would heal the man on the Sabbath – then they'd be able to accuse him. (**Have the groups on either side shade their eyes with their hand and stare at you intently.**) ³ Jesus said to the man whose hand was stiff and curled up: 'Get up and stand in the middle of us all.' (**Have the middle group stand, hands still curled and stiff.**) ⁴ And to the people watching him he said: 'Is it right to do good things on the Sabbath or bad things, to save life or to kill?' They didn't say a thing. (**Have the groups on the outside continue to stare and put a finger to their lips.**)

⁵ And he looked around at them angrily, really upset at how hard-hearted they were, and he said to the man: 'Stretch your hand out.' And he stretched it out and it was as good as new. (**Have the middle group slowly stretch out their hands, then cheer!**)

⁶ The Pharisees went out right away and began to plot against him with the Herodians to see if they could kill him. (**Have the outside groups turn to their neighbours and mutter angrily.**)

Lots of people came looking for Jesus

⁷ And Jesus went away with the disciples to the sea. (**Have everyone rock back and forth gently, like waves on the sea.**) And loads of people followed him (**now get everyone standing and walking in place, but do it bit by bit, one part of the crowd after another, as you read the place names**) – people from Galilee, ⁸ from Judea and Jerusalem, from Idumea, from the other side of the Jordan and the area up near Tyre and Sidon. Lots and lots of people heard what he was doing and came to him. (**Tell everyone to keep standing.**)

⁹ Jesus asked his disciples to get a small boat ready because of the crowd in case he was crushed. ¹⁰ And he healed many people (**have everyone cheer**) so that whoever had anything wrong with them at all pressed in and tried to touch him. ¹¹ And whenever troubled

spirits saw him, they fell down and shouted out loud (**have everyone shout the following line after you**): 'You are the Son of God.' [12] And Jesus really told them off, telling them not to reveal who he was.

Jesus chose 12 people

(**Divide your group into four: one for Peter, one for James and John, one for Simon from Cana, and one for Judas. Teach them the following lines before you read the passage. The Peter group make muscles and shout, 'You can call me Rocky!' The James and John group make a big, booming, thundery noise. The Simon group say in a James Bond-style voice, 'The name's Simon. Simon from Cana.' The Judas group hang their heads and say quietly, 'Yeah, I'm the one who betrayed Jesus.'**)

[13] Jesus went up the mountain and called the people he wanted to come with him, and they went to him. [14] He chose 12 to be with him, to go out and tell people his message [15] and to be able to send demons away. [16] So he chose the Twelve: these were Simon (he gave him the new name Peter) (**the Peter group**). [17] And James, the son of Zebedee, and John, James's brother (he gave them the name Boanerges, which means sons of thunder) (**the James and John group**). [18] And Andrew, and Philip and Bartholomew and Matthew and Thomas and James, Alphaeus' son, and Thaddeus and Simon

(the one who came from Cana) (**the Simon group**) ¹⁹ and Judas Iscariot (the one who betrayed Jesus) (**the Judas group**).

Family trouble

²⁰ Then Jesus went back home and the crowd came back again, so that this time he couldn't even eat. (**Have everyone shout, 'They say he has no time to eat!'**) ²¹ And when his family heard about it, they set out to grab him because some people were saying that he had lost his mind. (**Have everyone shout, 'They say that he's lost his mind!'**) ²² And the experts in the law who had come all the way from Jerusalem said, 'Beelzebul has hold of him,' and, 'He can drive off demons because he has the help of the prince of demons.' (**Have everyone shout, 'They say that he works for the devil!'**) ²³ And he called them over and said to them in stories: 'How can the devil drive off the devil? ²⁴ A country that is split down the middle cannot survive. (**Now split your group right down the middle. Have one side wave their fists at the other and shout angrily, 'We can't work with you!' And have the other side shout back, 'And we can't work with you, either!'**) ²⁵ And if a family is split down the middle, it can't survive. (**Now, do that again!**) ²⁶ And if the devil has risen against himself and is split down the middle, he can't survive either (**now, do it a third time!**) – it will be the end of him. ²⁷ No one can go into a strong man's house and steal his stuff (**have everyone, in both groups, make a muscle and shout, 'You**

can't take my stuff!') unless he's been tied up first, then you can go in and steal whatever you like. (**Now, have everyone hold their wrists together or wrap their arms around themselves, as if they are tied up, and mutter, 'Oh, yeah, now you can.'**)

[28] 'Listen carefully when I tell you that people will be forgiven for everything they've done wrong and everything they've said against God. (**Have everyone cheer.**) [29] But if anyone says anything against the Holy Spirit, that person will never be forgiven but will be guilty of having done something wrong – for ever.' (**Have everyone say, 'Oh, dear, but what does that mean?'**) [30] He said this because they kept on saying that he had an evil spirit.

(**Divide your group along gender lines. Women hold up one hand and say, 'I'm your mother!' Men hold up one hand and say, 'I'm your brother!'**) [31] His mother (**W**) and brothers (**M**) arrived and stood outside. [32] They sent a message asking him to come. There were a lot of people sitting around him and they told him, 'Your mother (**W**) and brothers (**M**) are outside looking for you.' [33] He said to them, 'Who is my mother? (**W**) Who are my brothers?' (**M**) [34] He looked at the people sitting around him in a circle and said, 'Here are my mothers (**W**) and my brothers (**M**). [35] Anyone who does what my Father wants, that person is my brother (**M**) and sister and mother (**W**).'

Mark 4

A story about sowing and growing

¹ And Jesus began to teach again by the sea (**have everyone rock back and forth, like waves on the sea**) and such a huge crowd gathered around him that they pushed a boat out into the sea (**more sea rocking**) and he sat in it. And the whole crowd was by the sea (**and a bit more rocking**) on the land. ² And he told them many things using stories, and one of the things he said was this.

(**For the next section, divide your group into four. Those in Group 1 pretend to be birds, gobbling up seeds. Those in Group 2 stand up when the seed springs up, then wither away with a sad sigh and sink back into their chairs. Those in Group 3 put their hands around their throats and make a choking sound. Those in Group 4 stand taller and taller still, throw their arms into the air and shout, 'Hooray!' or 'Woohoo!' or whatever they like! Of course, you can also have everyone do every action, if you like.**)

³ 'Listen carefully. **(Have everyone put their hand to their ear, as if listening.)** Someone went out to sow seed. ⁴ As he was scattering the seed, some of it fell on the side of the road and the birds came and ate it **(Group 1)**. ⁵ Other seeds fell on ground with lots of stones in it and they sprang up straight away **(Group 2 springs up)**, because the soil wasn't very deep. ⁶ When the sun came up, they were scorched and, because they had no roots, withered and died **(Group 2 dies)**. ⁷ Other seeds fell into the middle of a patch of thorny plants, and the thorny plants choked them, and produced no grain **(Group 3)**, ⁸ but other seeds fell on good soil and they grew and grew and grew and produced lots of grain, some 30 times, some 60 and some 100 times more than the sower planted **(Group 4)**.

⁹ 'Let the people who can, listen **(hand to ear again)** carefully and work out what this means.'

¹⁰ As soon as Jesus was on his own, those with him, including the 12 disciples, began asking him about his stories. ¹¹ And he said to them: 'The key to the mystery of God's kingdom has been given to you, but for those on the outside, all they have is stories. ¹² This means that they can look and look **(have everyone put their hand above their eyes in a looking into the distance motion)** and just can't see

anything; they can listen and listen (**hand to ear again**) and have no idea what is going on – if they did they would turn and be forgiven.'

[13] And he said to them: 'Surely you know what this story's about? If you don't, how will you understand all the other stories?

[14] 'The person sowing seed is sowing God's message. [15] The seeds that fall on the side of the road are the people who, when the sower sows God's message, the devil comes straight away and takes the message that was sowed (**Group 1**). [16] And the seeds sowed on the ground with lots of stones in it are the people who hear the message and, as soon as they hear it, are very happy with it (**Group 2 springs up**). [17] But they aren't rooted properly and only last a short time; when really hard things happen because of the message they've heard, they give up and go away (**Group 2 dies**). [18] Others are the ones sown in the middle of a patch of thorny plants. These ones hear God's message, [19] but the worries of their everyday lives, the attractions of being rich and all the other things they want crowd around and choke out God's message (**Group 3**) so that what it says leads to nothing. [20] But other people are the seeds sown in good soil; they hear God's message, accept and bear fruit, some 30 times, others 60 times and others 100 times more than was sown' (**Group 4**).

What is God's kingdom like?

[21] And Jesus said to them: 'You don't get a lamp and put it in a large pot or under a bed, do you? [22] You hide something only so you can show it off later (**have everyone hold their hands in front of them, as if they are hiding something, then take their hands away and shout 'Surprise!'**); you keep a secret only so you can tell people about it later. (**Do the surprise thing again!**) [23] Let the people who can, listen (**hand to ear again**) carefully and work out what this means.'

[24] He kept on saying to them: 'Be careful what you listen to (**hand to ear**). What you give is what you get . . . and even more. (**Pretend to give something away with one hand, then take it back with the other.**) [25] The person who already has will get more (**do the surprise thing again**) and for the person who doesn't have, even what they have will be taken away.' (**Everyone scratches their heads and looks at each other with confusion.**)

[26] He went on to say: "The kingdom of God is like a person who plants seeds on some soil. (**Have everyone pretend to plant seeds.**) [27] This person goes to sleep and gets up (**have everyone make a head-in-hands, sleeping, snoring motion, followed by a hands-in-air, stretching, yawning, waking-up motion**), day (**repeat that set of motions**) after day (**repeat it again!**) – the seed sprouts and

grows and the person has no idea how. (**Have everyone scratch their heads.**) ²⁸ The soil produces grains all by itself – first the stem and then the grains on the top of the stem and then the full ears of wheat. (**Have everyone look down, and then further up, and further up, watching the plant grow.**) ²⁹ Whenever the crop is ready, straight away the person takes a sickle because the harvest is ready.' (**Have everyone grab a pretend sickle and swing it about.**)

³⁰ Jesus said: 'What is the kingdom of God like? What stories can we tell about it?

³¹ 'It is like a mustard seed that is sown in the soil; it is the tiniest of all seeds on the Earth. (**Everyone hunches over and makes themselves very small.**) ³² But when it is sown, it grows and grows and becomes the biggest plant of all. (**From hunched position, start straightening up to make yourself bigger and bigger.**) It even makes huge branches so that the birds of the air can rest in its shade.' (**Have everyone flap their wings and make whatever bird sound they like.**)

³³ He spoke to them with many stories like this, as many they were able to understand. ³⁴ He didn't speak without stories but he explained everything in secret to his disciples. (**Do the surprise motion, one last time.**)

A terrifying storm

³⁵ That day, when it started getting dark, Jesus said: 'Why don't we go over to the other side of the sea?' (**Have everyone do that gentle, rocking-back-and-forth sea motion.**) ³⁶ They left the crowd behind and took Jesus, just as he was, in the boat (**more gentle sea rocking**). There were other boats with him. ³⁷ A massive windy gale appeared (**have everyone wave their hands in front of them, back and forth, and make a blowy wind sound**) and the waves crashed over the boat (**have everyone wave their hands up and down and make a whooshing sound with a wave motion**), so that it wasn't long before the boat was full of water. ³⁸ Jesus was asleep on a cushion at the back of the boat (**have everyone make a snoring sound**) and they woke him up and said to him (**have everyone repeat the following line after you**): 'Teacher, don't you care that we're about to die?' ³⁹ Jesus woke up, sternly told off the wind and said to the sea: 'Be quiet! Be completely still!' The wind stopped and there was a great stillness. (**Have everyone stand completely still.**) ⁴⁰ Jesus said: 'Why are you so easily scared? Haven't you got any faith?' ⁴¹ Then they were really, really frightened and said to each other (**with trembling voices, have everyone repeat the following lines after you**): 'Who is this? Even the wind and the sea listen to him.'

Mark 5

Jesus, a healing and some pigs

(Divide your group into two. Group 1 will do the actions for the man with the troubling spirit. Group 2 will do the pig actions. Alternatively, you can just have everyone do all the actions.)

[1] Jesus and his disciples arrived at the other side of the sea, in the country of the Gerasenes. [2] When Jesus got out of the boat, right away a man with a troubled spirit came up to him from the cemetery. [3] He lived among the tombs and no one was able to restrain him any more, not even with a chain. (**Have Group 1 hold both arms in the air, fists together, clenched, then move their arms apart, suddenly, as if breaking chains holding them.**) [4] He had often been chained up, with chains around his feet and hands, but he'd smashed the chains and no one was strong enough to control him. (**Group 1 repeats breaking chains motion.**) [5] The whole time, day or night, he wandered among the graves and on the mountains, shouting and cutting himself with stones. (**Group 1 does the breaking chains motion again.**)

⁶ He saw Jesus from a distance and he ran to him and started worshipping him. (**Have Group 1 make a bowing motion.**) ⁷ He shouted really loudly, 'What have you got to do with me, Jesus, son of the Most High? I'm begging you, don't torment me.' ⁸ He said this because Jesus had said: 'Come out of him, you troubling spirit.' ⁹ Jesus asked him: 'What's your name?' He said, 'I'm called Legion because there are lots of us.' ¹⁰ And he started begging Jesus not to send him out of the country. (**Have Group 1 clasp their hands together in a begging motion.**)

¹¹ There happened to be a large herd of pigs feeding there on the mountain. (**Have Group 2 make a piggy nose and snorting pig sounds.**) ¹² The spirits begged Jesus to send them into the pigs. (**Group 2 repeats pig sounds.**) ¹³ Jesus allowed them, so the troubling spirits went into the pigs (**more pig sounds from Group 2**). The herd rushed over a cliff and into the sea (**pig sounds from Group 2 and then a long 'Aaaaaaah!'**) – there were about 2,000 of them and they all drowned in the sea (**pig sounds from Group 2, a bubbling noise as they go under water, a final 'Glug.'**) ¹⁴ The people looking after the pigs ran away and told everyone in the city and the fields around it and they all came to see what had happened. ¹⁵ They came to Jesus and saw the man who had been troubled by all those spirits sitting down, dressed

nicely and talking sensibly. (**Have Group 1 slick back their hair, smile and say, 'Hello.'**) They were really frightened. [16] The people who had seen what had happened told them all about the man with the spirits and about the pigs. (**Group 2 makes pig sounds, 'Aaaaaah' and 'Glug.'**) [17] They begged Jesus to get away from their area.

[18] Just as Jesus was getting into the boat again, the man who had been troubled by the spirits begged him to let him come too. (**Group 1 makes begging motion again.**) [19] But Jesus didn't let him. He said to him: 'Go home to your family and friends and tell them everything the Lord has done for you and how he showed kindness to you.' [20] And so the man went away and began telling everyone in the region of Decapolis (the place of the ten cities) the good news and what Jesus had done for him. (**Group 1 repeats breaking chain motion and says, 'Jesus broke my chains for good!'**) They were all really surprised.

A young girl and an old woman

(**Divide your group into three. Choose one person to play Jairus, but don't invite him to the front. Have him stay in the crowd, on one side of the room perhaps. Choose another person to play the ill woman. Again, have her stay in the crowd, perhaps on** the other side of the room. Everyone else should play the crowd. Ideally, everyone should stand throughout the whole of the story.)

²¹ Jesus crossed to the other side of the lake again and a big crowd gathered. (**Have everyone budge up to their neighbour, with a little jostling.**) He was by the sea. ²² A leader of the synagogue – called Jairus – saw him. He fell to his knees. ²³ He begged Jesus from his heart (**have the Jairus character make a begging motion and repeat the following lines after you**): 'My daughter is at death's door. Please come and lay hands on her so that she will get well again and live.' ²⁴ Jesus went with him.

A huge crowd followed and closed around them, pushing and shoving (**more crowd pushing and shoving**). ²⁵ A woman was there who had an illness that meant she had been bleeding for 12 years. (**Have the woman character say, in a weak voice, 'I'm so ill.'**) ²⁶ She'd spent every last penny on doctors, but she hadn't got any better – in fact, she'd got worse. ²⁷ She'd heard about Jesus so she came up behind him in the crowd and touched his cloak (**have the woman character reach out and gently touch the clothes of someone standing near her**) ²⁸ because she thought to herself, 'If I can just touch his cloak, I will be freed from all of this.' ²⁹ Right away, the bleeding stopped and she could feel in her body that she was better from her illness. (**Have the woman whisper, 'I'm healed! I really am!'**) ³⁰ Right away, Jesus could feel that the power had gone out of him; turning to the crowd, he said: 'Who touched my cloak?' ³¹ His disciples said to him: 'Look at the crowd, pushing and shoving around you (**more crowd pushing and shoving**) and you say, "Who touched me?" ³² Jesus looked around trying to see the woman who had done this. ³³ The woman, terrified and shaking all over (**have the woman shake and then bow**), knowing what had happened to her, fell down in front of him and told him everything. ³⁴ And he said to her: 'Daughter, your faith has saved you; go in peace and be whole, free from your illness.'

³⁵ While he was still speaking, some people came from the house of the leader of the synagogue and said to Jairus: 'Your daughter has died. (**Have Jairus cry out, 'Oh, no, my daughter's dead!'**) Why bother the teacher any more?' ³⁶ But Jesus overheard what they were saying and said to the leader of the synagogue: 'Don't be afraid, just believe.' ³⁷ And he wouldn't let anyone follow him except for Peter, James and John, the brother of James. ³⁸ When he got to the leader of the synagogue's house, he saw an uproar – lots of people were crying and weeping really loudly. (**Have the crowd pretend to weep loudly.**) ³⁹ He went in and said: 'Why are you making such a scene and crying? The child hasn't died, she's just asleep.' ⁴⁰ They

started laughing at him (**have the crowd laugh loudly**), but he threw them all out. He just took the child's father and mother, and those he'd brought with him, and went into the place where the child was. ⁴¹ He took the child by her hand and said: 'Talitha kum!' (which, if you translate it, means 'Little girl, I tell you, get up'). ⁴² Right away, the girl got up and walked around – she was about 12 years old – and they were totally astonished. (**Have Jairus shout, 'Yes, my daughter's alive!'**) ⁴³ He gave them a talking to about how no one should know anything about this, and he told them to give her something to eat.

Mark 6

Jesus went home

[1] Jesus left there and came to the town he grew up in. (**Have everyone wave to each other and shout, 'Welcome to Nazareth! Population 400! Where everybody knows everybody!'**) His disciples followed him. [2] When the Sabbath came he began to teach in the synagogue and lots of those listening to him were stunned and said (**have everyone put their hand to their mouth and whisper the following sentences, one by one, to a neighbour after you, in a surprised and slightly suspicious fashion**): 'Where did he get all this? How did he get to be so wise? And where did the miracles he does with his own hands come from? [3] Isn't he the carpenter – the son of Mary and the brother of James, Joses, Judas and Simon? And aren't those his sisters who are here with us?' And they were really put out by him. (**Have everyone cross their arms and grumble, 'Just who does he think he is?'**) [4] Jesus said to them: 'A prophet gets respect but not in the place he grew up, nor among the people who have always known him, nor at home.' [5] And he wasn't able to do any miracles there except for a few sick

30

people whom he laid hands on and healed. (**Have everyone cross arms again and grumble, 'See, what did we tell you?'**) [6] He was surprised by them not believing.

Jesus sent the Twelve out

(**In this passage, your group will be playing 'the Twelve'. You might want to introduce it that way.**)

He went round teaching in the villages. [7] He called the Twelve and began to send them out, two by two (**have each person link an arm with a neighbour**) and he gave them power over the troubling spirits that would get in their way (**have everyone strike a superhero pose**). [8] He told them not to take anything with them for the journey, except for a walking stick (**have everyone look at their linked neighbour and say in a surprised fashion, 'Whaaaat?'**) – they weren't to take a bag (**have everyone look at their neighbour and say, 'No bag?'**), bread (**keep looking at that neighbour and say, 'No bread?'**) or even money in a belt around their waist (**to that neighbour again, 'No money?'**) [9] They should wear sandals, but not wear extra clothes (**say to the neighbour, 'You're gonna smell!'**) [10] He said to them: 'Whenever you go into a house, stay there until you leave again (**have everyone say, 'Home, sweet, home!'**) [11] If you're not welcome somewhere and they just won't listen to you, shake your feet as you leave as a sign that you're leaving it all behind' (**have everyone shake the dust off their feet**). [12] So the Twelve went out and told people the good news, that they could turn their lives around (**have everyone shout, 'Good news!'**) [13] And they got rid of loads of demons and they anointed lots of ill people with oil, so that they were healed (**have everyone strike a superhero pose**).

King Herod killed John the Baptist

(**Divide your group into three, one for Herod on one side, one for Herodias on the other side and one for their daughter in the middle.**)

[14] King Herod had heard of it. Jesus' name had become famous and people kept saying he was John, the one who baptized people, risen from the dead and this was why miracles kept on happening with him. [15] Others said, 'He's Elijah,' and others said, 'He's a prophet like those who used to live a long time ago.' [16] But Herod, when he heard about it, kept on saying (**have the Herod group repeat the following lines after you, in a surprised and slightly worried fashion**): 'John, the one who baptized people, whose head I had cut off – he's come back to life again!'

[17] Herod had sent people to arrest John and threw him in prison because of Herodias (she was his brother Philip's wife but Herod

had married her) (**have the Herodias group shrug and say, 'It's complicated'**). ¹⁸ And John had been telling Herod that you aren't allowed to marry your brother's wife. ¹⁹ Herodias held a grudge against John (**have the Herodias group mutter, 'I hate that guy!'**) and wanted to kill him, but she couldn't (**have the Herodias group grumble, 'It's so frustrating!'**) ²⁰ because Herod was afraid of John, knowing that he was in the right and blessed by God and looked after by him. Every time he heard him speak he was really worried (**have the Herod group say, 'He worries me'**), but he still liked listening to him (**the Herod group says, 'But I like him'**).

²¹ Then one day there was a perfect opening (**have the Herodias group rub their hands together and laugh villainously, 'Mwah-hah-ha!'**) – it was Herod's birthday and he had a huge party for all the important people in his court, as well as for the leaders of the army and other leaders in Galilee (**have the Herod group do a little dance and say, 'Party time for me and my posse!'**) ²² When his and Herodias' daughter came in and danced (**have the Daughter group do a little dance, the sillier the better. You might want to demonstrate!**), she pleased Herod and his guests so much that the King said to the girl: 'Ask me for anything and I'll give it to you.' ²³ He promised her that whatever she asked for – even half his kingdom – he would give her. (**The Herod group turns to**

the Daughter group and says, 'I'll give you what you want, even half my kingdom!') ²⁴ She went out and said to her mum: 'What shall I ask for?' (**The Daughter group repeats this.**) She said (**have the Herodias group do that villainous laugh and hand-rubbing again, then repeat the answer after you**): 'The head of John, the one who baptizes people.' ²⁵ The girl sped back to the King right away and asked: 'I want you to give me the head of John, the one who baptizes people.' (**The Daughter group repeats this.**) ²⁶ The King was really upset (**have the Herod group shout 'Whaaat?' in a surprised and disgusted fashion**), but because of his promise (and the guests), he didn't want to say no. (**Have the Herod group shrug and say, 'Ah, well.'**) ²⁷ Right away, the King sent a soldier with a very sharp sword and orders to bring John's head. So he went and chopped off John's head in the prison. ²⁸ He brought his head on a plate and gave it to the girl. (**Have the Herod group make disgusted faces and pretend to hand the plate with the head to the Daughter group.**) The girl gave it to her mum. (**Have the Daughter group repeat Herod's actions and hand the plate to the Herodias group. Then have the Herodias group do the nasty laugh and hand-rubbing again.**) ²⁹ When his disciples heard about it, they came and took his body away and laid it in a tomb. (**Then the leader says, 'Because as much as this feels like a ridiculous and sad pantomime, it resulted in the death of God's chosen prophet.**

And that was something to be truly sad about. So let's leave our characters behind and join with the disciples and carry John's body to the tomb.' Then have everyone pretend to hold that body in their arms and finish with sad, bowed heads.)

Jesus and his disciples tried to have a rest . . .

(Divide your group into two. One group will play the disciples, the other will play the crowds that followed them.)

30 And the people he'd sent out gathered together around Jesus and told him everything that they had done and taught. (**Have the Disciple group hold out their hands, as if explaining, and shout, 'It was amazing!'**) 31 Jesus said to them: 'Come away to a quiet place and have a bit of a rest.' (**Have the Disciple group wipe their foreheads and say, 'Phew!'**) Because lots of people kept coming and going, so that they hadn't even got time to have something to eat. (**Have the Disciple group moan, 'We're famished!'**) 32 And they went away by boat, to a place in the desert by themselves. (**Have the Disciple group make a rowing motion.**)

33 But people saw them going and recognized them (**have the Crowd group stand and look with hand over eyes and shout, 'That's them! They're getting away!'**) and raced there on foot from

all the different towns (**have the Crowd group run in place**) and got there before them. (**Have the Crowd group throw their hands in air and shout, 'Winners!'**) [34] Jesus got out of the boat and saw an enormous crowd (**have the Crowd group wave and shout, 'Hi, Jesus!'**) and he felt for them deeply, because they were like sheep with no shepherd (**have the Crowd group say a sad little 'Baaa'**) and he began to teach them about all sorts of things.

. . . but fed five thousand people instead

[35] It got late and his disciples came to him and said (**have the Disciple group hold out their hands and repeat the following lines, sentence by sentence, after you**): 'This place is in the middle of nowhere and it's really late. [36] Send these people away so that they can go into the fields and villages near here and buy themselves something to eat.' [37] But he answered them: 'You give them something to eat.' And they said (**have the Disciple group shout in an incredulous manner, 'Whaaat?'**), 'Do you really want us to go away and buy bread that's a *lot* of money (two hundred denarii worth) and give it to them to eat?' [38] And he said to them, 'How many loaves have you got? Go and find out.' When they knew, they said (**have the Disciple group hold up five fingers on one hand and two on the other and repeat their line after you**): 'Five loaves and two fish.' [39] Jesus told them all to sit down group

by group on the pale green grass. **(Have the Crowd group say to one another, 'Let's sit down in groups!')** [40] And they sat down, making lots of colourful groups in 100s and 50s. **(Have the Crowd group remark to one another, 'You're looking very colourful!')** [41] Jesus picked up the five loaves of bread and two fish and looked up towards heaven. He blessed it and broke the bread into pieces and gave it to his disciples so that they could give it out. And he divided the two fish among them all as well. [42] And everyone ate until they were really full. **(Have the Crowd group make noisy gobbling-up sounds and motions and then burp.)** [43] They filled up 12 big baskets with the leftover pieces of bread and fish. [44] Five thousand men ate the bread. **(Have the Crowd group shout, 'And thousands of women and children, too!')**

[45] Right away, he made his disciples get into a boat **(have the Disciple group repeat the rowing motion and say, 'Here we go, again!' Tell them to keep rowing as you tell the rest of this story)** and go ahead of him to the other side (to Bethsaida) while he let the crowd go home **(have the Crowd group wave and say, 'Bye-bye!')** [46] When he'd said goodbye, he went to a mountain to pray. [47] When evening came, the boat was in the middle of the sea **(have the Disciple group keep rowing and wipe foreheads with a 'Phew!')** and Jesus was alone on the land. [48] He saw them painfully struggling to row

because there was a wind blowing against them. (**Have the Disciple group keep rowing and shout, 'We're exhausted!'**) In the early morning, he came to them walking on the sea and he wanted to pass them by. ⁴⁹ But when they saw him walking on the sea, they thought that he was a ghost and screamed (**have the Disciple group keep on rowing and scream, 'It's a ghost!'**) ⁵⁰ because they all saw him and were terrified. Right away, he spoke to them and said: 'Be brave, it's me, don't be afraid.' ⁵¹ He got into the boat with them and the wind dropped. They were totally astonished (**have the Disciple group stop rowing and simply say, 'Whoah. What was that all about?'**) ⁵² because they didn't understand and they were hard-hearted.

⁵³ And crossing over to the land (**the Disciple group rows some more**) they came to Gennesaret and tied the boat up. ⁵⁴ When they got out of the boat, people recognized Jesus right away (**have the Crowd group shout, 'Look, it's Jesus! He's come to visit us, too!'**) ⁵⁵ and raced around that whole area and began to carry ill people on mats to him wherever they heard that he was. (**Have the Crowd group run in place and pretend to carry someone.**) ⁵⁶ And everywhere when he went into villages or cities or farms, they used to put the sick in marketplaces (where everyone gathered) (**have the Crowd group pretend to set their passenger down**) and beg

him to let them touch the edge of his cloak. And everyone who did touch it was healed. (**Have the Crowd group shout, 'We're healed!'**)

Mark 7

Being clean on the inside or the outside

[1] Some Pharisees and some of the scribes (who came from Jerusalem) gathered around Jesus [2] and they saw that some of his disciples were eating bread with unclean hands (in other words, without washing them first). **(Everyone looks at their hands in shock and shouts, 'Dirty!' or 'Ewwww!')** [3] Pharisees (and all the rest of the Jews) never eat without a hand-washing ceremony **(everyone pretends to wash their hands in a really vigorous manner)**, which is what the elders passed down to them [4] *and*, whenever they come in from the marketplace, they don't eat until they've washed themselves from top to toe **(everyone pretends to wash themselves, in a vigorous manner again, from head to foot)**, and there are many other things that have been passed down which they do too, such as washing cups and jugs and copper pots **(pretend to clean something)** – [5] so when they saw this, the Pharisees and scribes asked: 'Why do your disciples not follow the traditions that have been passed down to us from the elders but eat their food with unclean hands?' **(Everyone looks at their hands again and shouts, 'Dirty!' or 'Ewww!')**

⁶ And Jesus said, 'Isaiah prophesied about two-faced people like you (**everyone points to one side of their face and says, 'One face!', then quickly turns their head and points to the other side and says, 'Two face!'**) when he wrote, "This people respects me with their lips (**everyone points a finger at their lips**), but their hearts are far, far away from me (**everyone pretends to grab hold of heart through chest and fling it far away**). ⁷ Their worship is pointless, they teach things that human beings have made up as though they are something that you need to believe. ⁸ You've let go of God's commandments and picked up human traditions instead."' (**Everyone pretends to let something drop from one hand, then bends down and picks up something with the other hand.**)

⁹ He also said to them: 'You have a fine way of throwing away God's commands (**everyone pretends to fling something away with one hand**) so that you can set up your own traditions (**everyone pretends to stack up bricks with the other hand**). ¹⁰ Moses said: "Respect your father and your mother" (**everyone opens arms wide and says, 'Love ya, Ma! Love ya, Pa!'**) and "Anyone who insults his father and mother should die." ¹¹ But you say, "If someone says to his father or his mother that anything they might have had from him is Corban" (which means a gift set apart for God), ¹² then you no longer let him do anything for his father or

his mother. (**Everyone folds their arms across their chest and says, 'Tough luck, Ma. Tough luck, Pa.'**) [13] This cancels God's word (**everyone makes an X with their arms in front of their chest**) with your own traditions that you have handed down (**everyone pretends to pass something to their neighbour**). You do lots of things like this.'

[14] Jesus called the crowd to him again and said to them: 'Everyone listen to me (**everyone holds a hand to their ear**) and make sure you understand (**everyone points a finger to their head**). [15] There isn't anything outside someone that, if it goes into them, can make them unclean (**everyone pretends to pluck something from the air and swallow it, then says, 'Still clean!'**); it is what comes out of someone that makes them unclean.' (**Everyone pretends to pull something out of their mouths, looks at it and says, 'Dirty!' or 'Ewwww!'**) [17] He went away from the crowd and into a house and his disciples asked him about the story. [18] And he said to them, 'Don't you understand either? Surely you get that what goes into someone from the outside just can't make them unclean? (**Everyone pretends to pluck something from the air and swallow it, then says, 'Still clean!'**) [19] It doesn't go into their heart but into their stomach and out again into the toilet.' (**Everyone pretends to flush a toilet and makes that flushing sound!**) (This meant that he said all food was clean.)

²⁰ He carried on: 'It's what comes out of someone that makes them unclean. (**Everyone pretends to pull something out of their mouths, looks at it and says, 'Dirty!' or 'Ewww!'**) ²¹ Evil ideas come from the inside, from the heart of someone, things like (**as each of the following evil actions is listed, have everyone pretend to pull out something from their mouths, give it a disgusted look, and chuck it away**) having sex with someone you shouldn't; stealing things; killing people; ²² cheating on someone; wanting something that someone else has got; nastiness; tricking people; doing whatever you want; being jealous; saying horrible things; being arrogant or silly. ²³ All these evil things come from the inside. They are what make you unclean.' (**Everyone pretends to pull something out of their mouths, looks at it and says, 'Dirty!' or 'Ewww!'**)

A woman who wouldn't give up

(**Split the group into two. Those in one group will play the role of the children and those in the other will play the role of the dogs.**)

²⁴ From there, Jesus went into the countryside near Tyre. He went into a house and didn't want anyone to know, but he wasn't able to keep it quiet. (**Everyone puts a finger to their lips and says, 'Shhhh!'**) ²⁵ Right away, a woman heard about him – her

43

daughter had a troubled spirit. The woman came to him and fell flat on her face in front of him. (**Everyone stretches their hands out before them and bows their head.**) [26] She was Greek, born in Syrophoenicia, and she begged him to get rid of the demon in her daughter. (**Everyone makes a begging, pleading motion.**) [27] But Jesus said to her: 'Let the children eat first until they are full (**the Children group noisily gobbles down food**) because it just isn't right to take bread away from children and throw it to the dogs.' (**Now you pretend to grab the food away from the Children side of the room and throw it to the Dogs group, which growls and snarls and wolfs down the food.**) [28] She answered and said: 'Yes, Lord, but even little dogs under the table (**more dog noises from the Dogs side**) get to eat the children's scraps.' (**The Children group pretends to drop food and says, 'Here you go, puppy!'**) [29] Jesus said to her: 'Because of what you just said, go on your way, the demon has left your daughter alone.' [30] She went back home; she found the child lying on her bed and the demon was long gone. (**Everyone lifts their hands in praise to God.**)

Jesus couldn't stop people talking about him

[31] Jesus went out again from Tyre and Sidon; he came to the sea of Galilee right in the middle of the Decapolis region. [32] They brought a man to him who was deaf (**everyone points at their ears and**

frowns) and found it hard to speak (**everyone sticks their tongue out and frowns, too**), and they begged him to lay his hands on him. ³³ He took the man away from the crowd into a private place, he put his fingers in the man's ears (**everyone puts their fingers on the edge of their ears**), spat and touched the man's tongue (**everyone pretends to spit on their hand and touch a finger to their tongue**). ³⁴ He looked up to heaven, gave a deep sigh and said to him: 'Ephphatha', which means, 'Open up'. ³⁵ Right away, the man's ears opened up (**everyone points at their ears and smiles**) and whatever was stopping his tongue was removed and he started speaking clearly (**everyone points at their tongue and smiles**). ³⁶ Jesus told them not to say anything to anyone (**everyone goes 'Shhhh!'**), but the more he told them not to (**have everyone shout, 'Jesus made me hear and speak!'**), the more they broadcast it. (**Everyone shouts, 'Jesus made me hear and speak!' over and over, and louder and louder and louder, again and again.**) ³⁷ They were stunned: 'He has done all these things so well – he makes those who can't hear, hear and those who can't speak, speak.'

Mark 8

(Divide your group into two – one group to be the crowd, the other the disciples.)

More hungry people – and (a lot) more food

[1] Around that time there was another huge crowd (**the Crowd group shouts, 'We're huge!'**) who had nothing to eat (**the Crowd group shouts, 'And we're hungry!'**) He called his disciples and said to them: [2] 'My heart goes out to this crowd because they've already stayed with me for three days (**the Crowd group shouts, 'Three! Three whole days!'**) and they've got nothing to eat (**'And we're still hungry!'**) [3] If I send them home hungry, they might pass out on the way (**the Crowd group shouts, 'We're already feeling woozy!'**) and some of them have come a really long way (**the Crowd group shouts, 'Miles and miles!'**) [4] And his disciples answered him (**the Disciple group shrugs, with a helpless or exasperated look on their faces and repeats the following lines after you**): 'How can anyone get enough bread to fill up these people? We are in the middle of nowhere!' [5] He kept on asking

them: 'How many loaves of bread have you got?' They said (**the Disciple group holds up seven fingers and repeats the following after you**): 'Seven.' [6] And he told the crowd to sit down on the ground and, taking the seven loaves of bread, he thanked God, broke them and gave them to his disciples to pass out, and they gave them to the crowd. (**If your group is small, tell the Disciple group to intermingle with the Crowd group and pass them pretend bread, which the Crowd group should then pretend to gobble up hungrily. If your group is large, tell the Disciple group to throw the pretend bread to the Crowd group, and they should then consume it hungrily.**) [7] They also had a few little fish. Jesus blessed these and said that they should be passed out too. (**Repeat the above action with the pretend fish. It might be fun for the Disciple group to shake their hands as if the fish are still wriggling, before handing them over!**) [8] They ate and got really full (**both groups burp**) – and there were seven big hampers of leftover pieces (**both groups shout, 'Leftovers!'**) [9] There were about 4,000 people there – and then Jesus sent them away.

On seeing and not seeing

(**Divide your group into two again, one group for the disciples, the other for the Pharisees.**)

¹⁰ And right away, Jesus got into a boat with his disciples (**the Disciple group turns to the left and rows in that direction**) and went to a place called Dalmanutha. ¹¹ And the Pharisees came out [from Jerusalem] and began to argue with him (**the Pharisee group raises fists and makes noisy arguing sounds**). They kept asking for a sign from heaven, trying to trip him up (**the Pharisee group points to the sky and shouts, 'Show us a sign from heaven!'**) ¹² And, heaving a huge sigh from deep within, he said: 'Why is this generation always looking for a sign? Listen carefully when I tell you that no sign will be given to this generation.' ¹³ And leaving them, he got in a boat again and went away to the other side (**the Disciple group turns to the right and rows in that direction**).

¹⁴ And they had forgotten to take any bread (they had nothing except for one loaf of bread with them in the boat). (**The Disciple group shouts, 'One loaf? For a six-hour journey? We're hungry!'**) ¹⁵ Jesus spoke to them seriously and said: 'Look out! Be careful of the yeast of the Pharisees and the yeast of Herod.' ¹⁶ And they started quarrelling with each other because they didn't have any bread. (**The Disciple group argues with one another, pointing and shouting, 'You forgot the bread! No, it's your fault!'**) ¹⁷ Jesus knew this and said to them: 'Why are you quarrelling about not having any bread? (**The Disciple group argues again, as above. Then they**

shake their heads, confused, after Jesus asks each of the following questions.) Haven't you noticed and understood yet? Are you still hard-hearted? [18] You've got eyes, can't you see? You've got ears, can't you hear? Don't you remember anything? [19] When I broke the five loaves for the 5,000, how many basketfuls did you take away?' They said (as though the light has just dawned, the Disciple group says, 'Ohhh! Now we get it. Twelve!'): 'Twelve.' [20] 'And when I broke the seven for the 4,000 how many big hampers full of broken pieces did you take away?' They said (the Disciple group says, 'Ohhh, now we get it! Seven!'): 'Seven.' [21] And he said to them: 'Do you understand yet?'

[22] And they came to Bethsaida. And they brought someone to him who was blind and begged him to touch him (everyone makes a begging motion). [23] He took the person who was blind by the hand and took him out of the village (everyone pairs up and takes the hand of the person next to them and walks in place). Jesus spat in his eyes and placed his hands on him (no, don't spit in the eyes of your neighbour! But do have one person in each pair place their hands over the eyes of their partner) and asked him: 'Can you see anything?' [24] The blind person looked up and said: 'I *am* looking at people, but I see them walking about like trees' (everyone stands, making themselves into a tree shape). [25] Then Jesus put his hands

on him again (**repeat the hands over the eyes motion**). He looked around carefully and could see again. He started seeing everything clearly. ²⁶ Jesus sent him home, saying: 'Don't even go into the village.'

Who was Jesus?

²⁷ Jesus and his disciples went into the villages around Caesarea Philippi, and on the way he asked his disciples, saying to them: 'Who are people saying that I am?' ²⁸ And they told him, saying 'John, the one who baptized people (**everyone makes a dunking motion and repeats 'John, the one who baptized people'**); and others say Elijah (**everyone makes a rain-with-fingers-that-suddently-stops motion and then repeats the name Elijah**), and yet others say (**everyone shouts, 'I speak for God' and then repeats the following line after you**) one of the prophets.' ²⁹ And he kept on asking them: 'And you, who do you say that I am?' Peter said to him: 'You are the Messiah.' ³⁰ And he warned them sternly not to tell anyone about him (**everyone puts a finger to their lips and goes 'Shhhhh!'**)

³¹ And he began to teach them that the Son of Man would suffer (**in an incredulous manner, everyone says, 'Suffer?'**) a lot of things and be declared useless by the elders and the chief priests and the

scribes (**in the same tone, everyone says, 'Useless?'**), and be killed (**everyone says, 'Killed?'**) and after three days rise again (**everyone says, 'Rise again?'**) [32] He said this really openly and Peter took him to one side and began to tell him off (**everyone says, 'Suffer? Useless? Killed? Rise again? No way!'**) [33] But Jesus turned and looked at his disciples and he told Peter off and said: 'Go away from me, you devil, because you aren't thinking about God's things but about human things.'

[34] Jesus called a crowd together with his disciples and said: 'Anyone who wants to follow me (**everyone walks in place**) needs to turn their back on themselves (**everyone turns round and walks the other way in place**), pick up their cross and follow me (**everyone turns back to the front, bends down, picks up cross, heaves it on their shoulder and keeps walking in place**). [35] For anyone who wants to save their life (**everyone pretends to grab hold of something and holds it tightly against their chest**) will lose it (**everyone drops that thing they have been holding tightly**), but anyone who loses their life for my sake (**now everyone drops that thing again**) and the sake of the gospel will save it (**now everyone picks it up again and holds it tightly**). [36] What good is it if you gain the whole world (**have everyone reach out high and low and all around, grabbing as much as possible**) but lose your life? (**Have**

them do the dropping thing again.) [37] What can you swap for your life? (**Everyone pretends to hold something in each hand and weigh them up.**) [38] Anyone from this faithless and wicked generation who is ashamed of me and my words, the Son of Man will be ashamed of, when he comes in his Father's glory with his angels.'

Mark 9

Jesus with Elijah and Moses

¹ Jesus said to them: 'Listen carefully (**everyone puts a hand to one ear and leans forward**) when I tell you that some people standing here will not experience death before they see the kingdom of God coming with power.' (**Everyone points to a neighbour and says, 'Who? You?'**)

² Six days later, Jesus took Peter, James and John and led them up a very big mountain. (**Everyone walks in place as if they are slowly climbing a mountain. Have them do this for a while. Encourage some wiping away of sweat and some huffing and puffing.**) They were all alone. What Jesus looked like changed before their eyes; ³ his clothes started shining bright white, whiter than anyone on earth would be able to bleach them (**everyone shouts, 'Whoah, that's whiter than white!'**) ⁴ Elijah appeared (**everyone shouts, 'Whoah, he's deader than dead!'**) along with Moses (**everyone shouts, 'Whoah, he's even deader!'**) and they started chatting with Jesus. ⁵ And Peter answered and said to Jesus: 'Rabbi, it's great to be

here **(everyone shrugs and says, 'A reasonable stab at an opening line')**. Why don't we make three tents – one for you, one for Moses and one for Elijah' **(everyone shrugs and says, 'A reasonable plan. Sounded good at the time')** ⁶ (because he didn't know *what* to say – they were all really scared). **(Everyone trembles and screams!)**

⁷ A cloud formed and covered them **(everyone covers their head with their hands)**. A voice came out of the cloud: 'This is my Son, I love him – listen to him' **(everyone leans forward again, in listening action)**. ⁸ Suddenly, looking around, they couldn't see anyone any more except for Jesus all by himself.

⁹ And as they came down the mountain Jesus asked them firmly not to describe to anyone what they had seen, until the Son of Man should rise from the dead. ¹⁰ They grasped what he said **(everyone nods and whispers, 'Whoah, we must be quieter than quiet')** but argued among themselves about what 'rising from the dead' meant. **(Everyone angrily shouts the following lines, one by one. 'He means it literally! He means it metaphorically! He means at the Last Day! And what does he mean by DEAD?')** ¹¹ They also asked him why the scribes say that Elijah must come first. **(Everyone scratches their head and asks, 'Why must Elijah come first?')** ¹² Jesus said to them: 'Elijah is coming first to make

everything new. So why is it written about the Son of Man that he would suffer a lot of things and would be treated as though he was of no importance? ¹³ But I tell you that Elijah has already come and they did to him whatever they wanted, as it is written about him.' **(Everyone shrugs and says, 'Whoah! And now we are more puzzled than ever!')**

A difficult case

(In this section, everyone plays the crowd/father.)

¹⁴ When they got back to the disciples, they saw a big crowd around them and some scribes arguing with them **(everyone raises fists and makes arguing sounds)**. ¹⁵ When the whole crowd saw Jesus they were really surprised and they ran to him to welcome him **(everyone waves and shouts, 'Hiya, Jesus!')** ¹⁶ Jesus asked: 'What were you arguing about with them?' ¹⁷ Someone in the crowd answered him: 'Teacher, I brought my son to you **(everyone clasps hands and holds them out in a negging position)**. He has a spirit that means he can't speak ¹⁸ and, whenever it seizes him, it throws him to the floor so that he foams at the mouth and grinds his teeth and his body goes completely stiff. I asked your disciples to throw the spirit out, but they weren't strong enough.' **(Everyone holds out their hands and shrugs, a helpless look on their face.)** ¹⁹ Jesus answered him and

said: 'This generation has no faith. How long am I going to be with you? How long do I have to put up with you? Bring him to me.'

²⁰ So they brought the boy (**everyone pretends to gently lead a boy by the arm**) and as soon as the spirit saw Jesus, it convulsed him and the boy fell on the ground, rolling around and foaming at the mouth. (**Everyone looks at the floor and cries, 'Oh, no!'**) ²¹ Jesus asked the boy's father: 'How long has this been happening like this?' And he said: 'Since he was a child. ²² Lots of times it has thrown him in the fire or into water, trying to kill him. If you can do something, help us, have pity on us.' (**Everyone makes a pleading motion.**) ²³ Jesus said: 'No, if *you* can. Everything is possible for someone who has faith.' ²⁴ Right away the child's father shouted: 'I do have faith; please help my lack of faith.' (**Everyone shouts, 'I do have faith; please help my lack of faith.'**)

²⁵ Jesus saw that a crowd was streaming together, so he told off the unclean spirit and said to it: 'You spirit, that is stopping this boy from hearing or speaking, I order you to get out and never come back again.' ²⁶ The spirit cried out and shook him from head to toe and then left. He became like a corpse, so much so that many people said that he was dead (**everyone cries out, 'Oh, no! He's dead!'**) ²⁷ But Jesus took him by the hand and raised him up, and he stood up (**everyone shouts, 'He's alive! He's free!'**) ²⁸ And when

they went into the house, the disciples asked him privately: 'Why couldn't we get rid of it?' ²⁹ And Jesus said: 'This type can only come out through prayer.'

Who is important?

³⁰ From there Jesus and his disciples went out and started going through Galilee, but he didn't want anyone to know. (**Everyone puts a finger to their lips and says, 'Shhhhh.'**) ³¹ He kept on teaching his disciples and said to them: 'The Son of Man is to be handed over into human control, and they will kill him. After he has been killed, he will rise again after three days.' ³² But they just didn't understand what he said (**everyone turns to their neighbour and whispers, 'I don't get it. I just don't get it!'**) and they were too scared to ask him. (**Everyone turns to their neighbour and whispers, 'You ask him. No, you ask him!'**)

³³ And they came to Capernaum, and in the house he began to ask them: 'What were you discussing on the way?' ³⁴ But they kept quiet because on the way they had been discussing who was most important (**everyone turns to their neighbour and whispers, 'You tell him. No, you tell him!'**) ³⁵ And sitting down, he called the Twelve and said to them: 'Anyone who wants to be first (**everyone turns to their neighbour and whispers, 'I want to be first!'**) must

be the last and servant of all.' (**Everyone turns to their neighbour and whispers, 'Really?'**) [36] He got a child to stand in the middle of them and, putting his arms around the child, he said: [37] 'Anyone who accepts a child like this one in my name accepts me, and anyone who accepts me doesn't just accept me but the One who sent me as well.'

And who is with us?

[38] John said to him: 'Teacher, we saw someone getting rid of demons in your name, but we stopped him (**everyone holds up their hand and shouts, 'Stop that!'**) because he doesn't follow us,' but Jesus said: [39] 'Don't stop him (**everyone shouts, 'My mistake. Carry on!'**) No one who does something miraculous in my name is able to say bad things about me quickly and easily. [40] Anyone who isn't against us is for us (**everyone shouts, 'If you're not against us, you're for us!'**) [41] Anyone who gives you a cup of water in my name because you belong to Christ (**everyone holds a pretend cup and shouts, 'Cheers!'**), listen to me carefully when I tell you that this person will not miss out on a reward.

(**Everyone stands for this next section.**)

[42] 'But if anyone makes one of these little ones, who believe, trip up in faith (**everyone pretends to trip**), they would be better off

having a heavy millstone put around their neck and being thrown into the sea (**everyone looks down and says, 'Oh, dear!'**)

[43] 'If your hand causes you to trip up in faith (**everyone looks at their hand, then pretends to trip again**), chop it off. You would be better off entering new life maimed than to go to Gehenna, into a fire that can never be put out, with two hands. [44/45] And if your foot causes you to trip up in faith (**everyone looks at their foot and pretends to trip again**), chop it off. You would be better off entering new life unable to walk than to be cast into Gehenna with two feet. [46/47] If your eye causes you to trip up in your faith (**everyone points to their eye and pretends to trip again**), throw it away. You would be better off entering the kingdom of God one-eyed than to be cast into Gehenna with two eyes, [48] where their maggot never dies and the fire can't be put out.

[49] 'For everyone will be seasoned with fire. [50] Salt is good (**everyone pretends to touch a bit of salt to the tongue and says, 'Yes, it is!'**), but if salt isn't salty any more (**everyone pretends to touch a bit of salt to the tongue and says, 'Yuck!'**), how will you make it salty again? (**Everyone shrugs and says, 'Dunno!'**) Have salt in yourselves and be at peace with each other.'

Mark 10

A tricky question

[1] And getting up he went from there to the Judea region, on the other side of the Jordan, and crowds came together again around him (**everyone waves and says, 'Hiya, Jesus!'**) and he began teaching them as he usually did. [2] And Pharisees came up, testing him and asking him whether a man can divorce his wife (**everyone crosses their arms and puts on a serious face and asks, 'Can a man divorce his wife?'**) [3] He responded and asked: 'What did Moses tell you to do?' [4] They said (**everyone crosses their arms and puts on that serious face again and says in a snarky fashion**): 'Moses allowed a man to write a notice of divorce and then send her away.' [5] Jesus said to them: 'He wrote this rule because you are so hard-hearted. [6] From the very start of creation, God made them male (**all males wave their hands**) and female (**all females wave their hands**). [7] This is why a man will leave his father and mother [8] and the two become one; then they are no longer two but one (**have married couples join their hands here**). [9] What God has joined together, no one should split apart.'

¹⁰ In the house the disciples started asking him about this (**everyone leans forward expectantly and says, 'Tell us more!'**) ¹¹ He said to them: 'If anyone divorces his wife and marries another one, he commits adultery against her. ¹² And if she divorces her husband and marries another one she commits adultery.'

Children are very important

¹³ They kept bringing children to him so that he could touch them but the disciples told off the people bringing them (**everyone stands and puts hands on hips and angrily says, 'Now, stop that!'**) ¹⁴ But when Jesus saw this he was outraged (**everyone stands and puts hands on hips again and says, 'Now, stop that!'**) and said to them: 'Let the children come to me; don't get in the way, for the kingdom of God belongs to people like this. ¹⁵ Listen carefully when I say to you: "Anyone who does not receive the kingdom like a young child will never ever enter it."' ¹⁶ And he put his arms around the children and blessed them with his hands. (**Have everyone reach out a hand above a child near them and pray a little blessing over them.**)

A hard challenge and a hard question

(You can do the following sections in one of two ways. You can divide your group into two, with one half for the young man and the other for the disciples, or you can have everyone do everything.)

[17] He was just setting out on a journey when a man ran up to him (**everyone runs in place**) and fell on his knees (**everyone falls to their knees, if possible or appropriate, or just sits back down on their seat, hands extended**) and asked him (**everyone repeats the following line**): 'Good teacher, what do I need to do to inherit eternal life?' [18] And Jesus said to him: 'Why are you calling me good? No one is good except for God. [19] You know the commandments – don't kill people; don't be unfaithful in your relationships; don't steal things; don't say things that aren't true; don't cheat; give your respect to your mother and father.' [20] The man said (**everyone repeats the following line**): 'Teacher, I have been careful to do all of these things since I was a young man.' [21] Jesus looked at him and his heart went out to him and he said: 'You are missing one thing – go, sell everything you've got and give the money to people who have nothing. You will have treasure in heaven; and then come follow me.' [22] The man was appalled at what Jesus said (**everyone shouts in disbelief, 'Whaaaat?'**) and he went away deeply upset because he had a lot of stuff. (**All shake their heads and sigh, 'But I really like my stuff!'**)

²³ And looking around, Jesus said to the disciples: 'It is really hard for those who are rich to enter the kingdom of God.' ²⁴ The disciples were startled at his words (**echoing the tone of the young man, everyone shouts in disbelief, 'Whaaaat?'**), but Jesus said to them again: 'Children, it is really hard to enter the kingdom of God. ²⁵ It is a lot easier for a camel to go through the eye of a needle (**everyone pretends to squeeze through a tight space**) than for a rich person to enter the kingdom of God.' ²⁶ The disciples were even more stunned at this (**repeat the 'Whaaaat?'**) and said to each other (**everyone turns to their neighbour and repeats the following line**): 'So who *can* be saved?' ²⁷ Jesus looked at them and said: 'It is impossible for human beings but not for God. For God everything is possible.' ²⁸ Peter said to him (**everyone repeats the following line**): 'Look, we left everything and followed you.' ²⁹ Jesus said: 'Listen carefully when I tell you that everyone who has left their house, their brother or sister, their mother or father or child or their livelihood for my sake and for the sake of the gospel ³⁰ will receive 100 times more houses, brothers, sisters, mothers, children and livelihoods (**everyone shouts, 'Woohoo!'**) – but they will come with persecutions in this age (**everyone sighs, 'Oh, dear'**) and eternal life in the age to come (**everyone shouts, 'Woohoo!' again**). ³¹ Many who are first will be last and the last first.'

Jesus startles his followers . . . again

[32] Jesus and his disciples were on the road going to Jerusalem. Jesus was walking ahead of them. They were startled (**everyone jump!**) and those following were afraid (**everyone tremble**). And taking the Twelve to one side again, he started to tell them what was about to happen. [33] He said: 'Look, we're going to Jerusalem and the Son of Man will be handed over to the chief priests and scribes, and they will give him a death sentence and hand him over to the Gentiles. [34] And they will make fun of him and whip him and kill him . . . and after three days he will rise again.'

(**Divide your group into two – one half for James, on your right, the other half for John, on your left.**)

[35] James (**those in the James group put their hands up**) and John (**those in the John group put their hands up**), the sons of Zebedee, came up to Jesus and said (**everyone repeats the following line after you**): 'Teacher, we want you to do whatever we ask you to do.' [36] And Jesus said to them: 'What do you want me to do?' [37] They replied: 'Give us the right to sit in your glory, one on your right (**have those in the James group shout, 'I'm on your right!'**) and one on your left.' (**Have those in the John group shout, 'I'm on your left!'**)

[38] Jesus said: 'You have no idea what you are asking – are you strong enough to drink from the cup that I have to drink from? Or to be baptized with the baptism that I have to be baptized with?' [39] They said (**both groups repeat the following line after you, fists raised in the air like strong people**): 'We're strong enough.' So Jesus said to them: 'You will indeed drink from the cup that I drink from and be baptized with the baptism that I'm baptized with, [40] but sitting at my right and left hand is not for me to give. It is for the people it has been prepared for.' [41] When they heard this the other ten began to be outraged with James (**the James group puts their hand up**) and John (**the John group puts their hand up. Everyone shouts, 'Just who do you think you are?'**) [42] So Jesus called them and said to them: 'You know how those who are accepted as rulers of the Gentiles abuse their power and how the great oppress them? [43] It isn't to be like this with you. If anyone wants to be great among you (**the James group shouts, 'I want to be great!'**) they must be your servant (**the James group looks disappointed or surprised and says, 'Oh?'**) [44] And if anyone wants to be first (**the John group shouts, 'I want to be first!'**), they will be last (**the John group looks disappointed or surprised and says, 'Oh?'**) [45] Even the Son of Man didn't come to be looked after but to look after others and to give his life as the price that needs to be paid so that many people can be free.'

Jesus heals a blind man

(Divide your group into two, one half for the blind man, one half for the crowd.)

[46] They got to Jericho, and as Jesus and his disciples were leaving the city along with a large crowd of people, the son of Timaeus – Bartimaeus – a blind man who begged for a living, was sitting at the side of the road. [47] When he heard that it was Jesus of Nazareth he shouted out (**the Blind Man group shouts the following line after you**): 'Son of David, take pity on me.' [48] Many people told him to shut up (**the Crowd group shouts, 'Shut up!' or 'Be quiet!'**), but he shouted even louder (**the Blind Man group shouts the following line after you, even louder than before**): 'Son of David, take pity on me.' [49] Jesus stopped still and said: 'Call him here.' So they called the blind man and said (**the Crowd group shouts the following line after you**): 'Take heart, get up, he's calling you.' [50] He threw off his cloak, jumped up (**the Blind Man group pretends to throw off a cloak and jumps up from their seat**) and came to Jesus. [51] Jesus answered him and said: 'What do you want me to do for you?' The blind man said (**the Blind Man group repeats the following line after you**): 'Teacher, I want to see again.' [52] Jesus said to him: 'Go on your way, your faith saved you.' Right away he could see and followed Jesus along the road. (**Both groups shout, 'Hooray!!'**)

Mark 11

A donkey hunt, a procession . . .

(In this section, your group will pretend, mostly, to be the two disciples.)

¹ When they got close to Jerusalem, at Bethphage and Bethany on the Mount of Olives, Jesus sent two of his disciples (**everyone smiles and says, 'We're Disciples 1 and 2!'**) ² and said to them: 'Go into the village – the one that's right across from you – as soon as you get there you will see a young donkey tied up. No one has ever ridden it yet. Untie it and bring it. ³ And if anyone says to you: "What are you doing?" tell them, "The Lord needs it," and right away send it back here.' ⁴ And they went away (**everyone walks in place and says, 'Here we go!'**) and found the young donkey (**everyone points and says, 'Here's the donkey!'**) tied up outside on the street near a door and they untied it (**everyone pretends to untie a donkey and says, 'Now we're untying it!'**) ⁵ And some people who were standing around there said to them: 'What are you

doing, untying that young donkey?' [6] The disciples told them just what Jesus had said to say (**everyone smiles and says, 'Because the Lord needs it!'**) and they let them take it. [7] They brought the young donkey to Jesus (**everyone points and says, 'Here's your donkey, Jesus!'**) and laid cloaks over it. Jesus sat on it. [8] And many spread their cloaks on the road (**everyone pretends to spread cloaks on ground and shouts, 'We're spreading our cloaks!'**); others spread leafy branches they'd cut in the fields (**everyone pretends to spread branches and shouts, 'And leafy branches, too!'**) [9] The ones going in front and the ones following after shouted (**everyone shouts the following lines after you**): 'Hosanna! Blessed is the one who comes in the name of the Lord. [10] Blessed is the kingdom of our father David that is on the way. Hosanna in the Highest.'

. . . and a fig tree

[11] Jesus entered Jerusalem and entered the Temple. He looked around at everything. It was already late (**everyone pretends to look at wristwatch – or phone – and yawn!**), so he left for Bethany with the Twelve. [12] On the next day when they had left Bethany, he was hungry (**everyone rubs their tummy**). [13] And seeing a fig tree with leaves on from a long way off, he went to it to see if he could find something on it (**everyone pretends to look for figs on a pretend tree**). When he got to it he found nothing but leaves

(everyone shrugs and then sighs a disappointed sigh); it wasn't the time for figs (everyone looks at watch or phone again). [14] Jesus said to the tree: 'Let no one eat any fruit from you ever again.' His disciples heard him.

Jesus was really angry

[15] They came into Jerusalem. Jesus went into the Temple and started throwing out the people who were selling and buying in the Temple (everyone shouts, 'Hey, what are you doing?') and kicking over the tables of the people who changed the money into the coins they used in the Temple (everyone shouts, 'Hey, that's my money! What are you doing?') and the seats of the people selling doves (everyone shouts, 'Hey, those are my doves! What are you doing?') [16] He wouldn't even allow anyone to carry stuff through the Temple (everyone shouts, 'Hey, I need to get through. What are you doing?') [17] He started teaching and said to them: 'Isn't it written that "My house shall be called a house of prayer for all nations"? But you have made it into a place where robbers hide out.' [18] The chief priests and the scribes heard this and started looking for ways to do him in (everyone whispers to their neighbour, 'It's time we put an end to him!'); they were afraid of him because the whole crowd was stunned at his teaching [19] and whenever it was evening, they would go out of the city.

²⁰ Early in the morning they were passing the fig tree and saw that it was all dried up from the roots upward. ²¹ Peter was reminded of what had happened and said to Jesus (**everyone points and repeats the following line after you**): 'Teacher, look, the fig tree you cursed and dried up.' ²² Jesus answered and said: 'Have faith in God.'

Asking for things

²³ 'Listen carefully when I tell you that anyone who says to this mountain (**everyone makes the shape of a mountain with their arms and holds that pose**): "Be pulled up and thrown in the sea" and does not doubt in their heart but believes that what they say will happen, for that person it will happen (**everyone throws their mountain arms in the air and shouts, 'Whoah!'**) ²⁴ Because of this I tell you: Everything that you pray or ask for, believe that you have received it and it will happen (**everyone shouts, 'Whoah!' again**). ²⁵ When you stand praying, if you have anything against anyone, forgive them so that your Father in the heavens might also forgive you your sins.'

²⁷ They came to Jerusalem again. The chief priests, scribes and elders came to Jesus while he was walking around in the Temple. ²⁸ And they started saying to him (**everyone crosses their arms and looks quite angry and says the following lines after you**): 'What

right do you have to do these things? Who gave you the right to do them?' ²⁹ Jesus said to them: 'I am going to ask you one question. Answer me and I'll tell you what right I have to do these things. ³⁰ Answer me this: Was John's baptism from heaven or from human beings?' ³¹ They started debating among themselves (**everyone turns to their neighbour and mutters**): 'If we say "from heaven", he will say, "So why didn't you believe him, then?" ³² But should we say from human beings?' They were afraid of the crowd as they all thought that John really was a prophet. ³³ So they answered Jesus and said (**everyone shrugs and repeats the following line after you**): 'We don't know,' and Jesus said to them: 'So I won't tell you what right I have to do these things.'

Mark 12

A hard-hitting story

[1] Jesus started speaking to the people around him in parables.

(Divide your group into two – one half for the Vineyard Owner (VO), the other for the farmers (F).)

'A man planted a vineyard (the VO group pretends to jam vines into the ground). He put a fence around it (the VO group hammers a fence together), dug a pit to collect the juice from the winepress (the VO group digs a pit) and built a look-out tower (the VO group puts a hand above their eyes and pretends to be a look-out). He rented it out to some farmers and went abroad (the VO group pretends to be an aeroplane and shouts, 'Ibiza, here I come!') [2] When the moment came he sent a slave to the farmers so that he could get some of the fruit from the vineyard. [3] They took the slave, beat him up and sent him away empty-handed (the F group makes violent noises and then a throwing motion, as if throwing the slave out of the vineyard and back to the owner). [4] Again the owner sent another slave, but they hit him over the head and shamed him in public **(the F group repeats above actions)**. [5] He sent another and that one they killed **(the F group repeats above actions)**. He sent lots of others: some of them they beat up, others of them they killed **(the F group repeats above actions)**. [6] He only had one more person to send – a son that he really loved – he sent him last of all to them, saying to himself **(the VO group repeats the following line after you, nodding)**: "Surely they'll take notice of my son?"

[7] 'But those farmers pointed out to each other that he was the heir. **(The F group repeats the following lines to one another, in a conspiratorial fashion, after you.)** "Why don't we kill him?" they said, "and the inheritance will be ours." [8] So they took him, killed him and threw him out of the vineyard **(the F group repeats the the violent noise and throwing-out action)**. [9] What will the owner of the vineyard do? He will come and destroy the farmers and give the vineyard to other people. [10] Surely you've read the Scripture? "The stone that the house builders threw away **(the F group repeats the violent noise and, throwing-out action)** has become the stone that holds the whole building up **(the F group says, 'Uh-oh.')** [11] The Lord did this and in our view it is wonderful."' [12] They started looking for ways to catch him **(the F group repeats the**

conspiratorial muttering and you can even have them repeat the lines about killing the son, if you like), but they were frightened of the crowd. They knew that he had spoken the parables against them so they left him and went away.

A few trick questions . . .

(Divide your group into two – one half for the religious leaders (RL), the other for Jesus.)

[13] They sent some of the Pharisees and Herodians to him to catch him unawares by what he said (the RL group pretends to grab something or points a finger and shouts, 'Gotcha!') [14] They came to him and said: 'Teacher, we know that you are honest and don't care what anyone thinks, because you don't take sides and teach God's way truthfully. Is it right to pay taxes to Caesar? Shall we give them or not?' [15] Jesus knew that they were trying to trip him up (the RL group goes 'Gotcha!' again) and said to them: 'Why are you giving me a test? Bring me a denarius so that I can look at it.' [16] They brought one. And Jesus said: 'Whose picture and writing is this?' They said: 'Caesar's.' [17] Jesus said to them: 'Give to Caesar what belongs to Caesar and to God what belongs to God.' And they were totally baffled by him (the Jesus group goes 'Gotcha!')

(**Now divide your group into men and women. And, yeah, on the one hand, this is all about people dying, but, on the other, I thought it would be fun to do it in a ridiculous way to point out the ridiculous nature of the question.**)

[18] Some Sadducees came to him – they say that there is no such thing as resurrection (**everyone says, 'When you're dead, you're dead,' and then makes some kind of dying sound or action, possibly 'Aargh', then drops head to one side**) – and they asked him: [19] 'Teacher, Moses wrote for us that if a man happens to die (**Men dying motion again**) and leaves a wife but no child (**Women make sad face and sigh, or ridiculously loud wail**), his brother should marry the wife and have children for his brother (**the Men group turns to nearby women and either says, Joey Tribbiani-like, 'How you doing?' or falls on one knee, if possible, and says in a romantic tone, 'Will you marry me?'**) [20] Say there were seven brothers and the first got married (**Men, marry action**) and died (**Men, dying action**) leaving no offspring (**Women, sighing action**). [21] Then the second married her (**Men, marry action**) and died (**Men, dying action**) leaving no offspring (**Women, sighing action**) and the third . . . [22] say that the seven of them left no offspring (**Women, sighing action**) and in the end the woman died too (**Women, dying action**). [23] In the resurrection, whose wife will she be? All seven married her.'

²⁴ Jesus said to them: 'Isn't the reason that you have got this so wrong that you don't know the Scriptures or God's power? ²⁵ When people rise from the dead they won't marry or be given in marriage (**everyone shouts, 'Whaaaat?'**) – they'll be like angels in heaven (**everyone says, 'Oh!' in a slightly surprised fashion and flaps pretend wings**). ²⁶ Haven't you read in the book of Moses about the dead being raised, in the bit about the thorny bush where God spoke to him and said: "I am the God of Abraham and the God of Isaac and the God of Jacob." ²⁷ He isn't the God of the dead but of the living (**everyone shouts, 'So when you're dead, you're alive?' then cheers**). You have got it all completely wrong.'

. . . and some tricky questions

²⁸ One of the scribes came close and heard them arguing (**everyone makes arguing sounds**). He saw that Jesus gave good answers so he asked him: 'What commandment is the first of them all?' ²⁹ Jesus answered: 'The first one is: "Pay attention, Israel, the Lord our God is one (**everyone holds up their index finger**); ³⁰ you shall love the Lord your God with everything that you've got – your heart (**everyone puts their hand on their heart**), your life (**everyone puts their hand on their belly**), your mind (**everyone puts their hand on their head**) and your strength" (**everyone holds up their arms in a strong man pose**). ³¹ The second is: "Love your neighbour the way you love

yourself."' (**Everyone hugs a neighbour!**) [32] The scribe answered: 'That's a good answer; you are telling the truth when you say that "God is one (**index finger in the air again**) and there are no others apart from him" and [33] that "loving him with all that we've got – heart (**hand on heart**), life (**hand on belly**), mind (**hand on head**) and strength" (**strong man arms**) and that "loving your neighbour the way you love yourself" (**hug neighbour again**) is far more important than any burnt offering or sacrifice.' [34] Jesus recognized that he gave a thoughtful answer and said: 'You aren't far from God's kingdom.' Then no one dared ask him anything else. (**Everyone turns to a neighbour and mutters, 'I'm not asking him. You ask him.'**)

[35] Jesus was teaching in the Temple and asked: 'How can the scribes say that the Messiah is the son of David? [36] David himself, speaking by the power of the Holy Spirit, said: "The Lord said to my Lord, sit on my right until I put your enemies under your feet." [37] If David himself calls him Lord, how come he is his son?' The vast crowd listened to Jesus with huge enjoyment. (**Everyone turns to a neighbour and says, 'I'm enjoying this hugely!'**)

What God really values

(**Everyone will need to stand – if able – and pretend to be scribes for this next section.**)

³⁸ In his teaching Jesus also said: 'Be careful around the scribes who like to walk around in fancy robes (**everyone struts about like a model at a show**) and like people to greet them in the marketplace (**everyone waves and, in a phoney voice, says, 'Hello, hello. Lovely to see you, darling'**); ³⁹ or who like to have the best seats in the synagogue (**everyone points to self and says, 'For me?'**) and the place of honour at a party (**everyone says, 'You shouldn't have!'**) ⁴⁰ These kinds of people swallow up widow's houses (**everyone pretends to grab something and says, 'Sorry, you can't afford the payments . . .'**) and make a show of saying really long prayers (**everyone makes a show of folding hands, prayer-like, takes in a deep breath and then exhales, 'Really long prayer . . .'**). They will get greater than the average condemnation.' (**Everyone goes 'Whaaat? For me?'**)

⁴¹ Jesus sat down opposite the place in the Temple where people put their offerings. He watched carefully as the crowd put valuable objects in (**everyone hands over pretend stuff and says, smugly, 'See how generous I am!'**) and lots of rich people put vast riches in (**everyone repeats the action and says, 'See how good I am!'**) ⁴² Then a poor widow came and put in two small coins, which are hardly worth anything (**everyone whispers to their neighbour, 'See how little she's given . . .'**). ⁴³ Jesus called his disciples and said:

'Listen carefully when I tell you that this poor widow has put in more than everyone else. **(Everyone goes, 'Whaaat?')** [44] They gave out of the vast wealth they had but she, out of the very little that she had, gave everything she had to live on.' **(Everyone says, in a slightly embarrassed manner, 'Oh, I see.')**

Mark 13

Warnings

[1] Jesus was leaving the Temple and one of his disciples said to him: 'Teacher, look at these wonderful stones (**everyone pretends to stack up stones**) and wonderful buildings!' [2] Jesus said to him: 'Do you see these great buildings? There won't even be one stone left on another stone that hasn't been destroyed.' (**Everyone knocks down their stacked-up stones and makes a big crashing sound.**)

[3] Jesus was sitting on the Mount of Olives, opposite the Temple, and Peter, James, John and Andrew started asking him questions privately. [4/5] Jesus answered them and began to say: 'Be careful that no one fools you (**everyone says, 'You warned us. We won't be fooled'**). [6] Lots of people will come in my name and say: "I am the one" and lots of people will be fooled (**everyone says, 'You warned us. We won't be fooled'**). [7] When you hear about wars (**everyone shakes their fist and makes noisy warlike sounds**) and gossip about wars, don't be scared (**everyone says, 'You warned us. We won't be scared'**). These things have to happen but they aren't the end.

8 Nation will rise up against nation and kingdom against kingdom (**repeat warlike sounds**). There will be earthquakes in various places (**everyone shakes about as if in an earthquake and makes rumbling sounds**) and famines (**everyone puts hands on tummy and cries out, 'We're hungry!'**) but these are only the start of labour pains (**'You warned us. We won't be scared**). 9 But look out because they will hand you over to the courts and you'll be beaten in synagogues and you will stand before leaders and kings on account of me, as a witness to them (**'You warned us. We won't be scared'**). 10 But first the gospel must be preached to all nations (**everyone shouts, 'For God so loved the world!'**) 11 When they arrest you and hand you over, don't worry beforehand about what you're going to say but say whatever is given to you at that moment (**everyone says, 'You warned us. We won't be worried'**). You aren't the one speaking, it's the Holy Spirit. 12 Brother will hand over brother and a father will hand over his child and children will rise up against their parents and have them killed. 13 And you will be hated by everyone because of my name, but the person who holds on until the end will be saved (**'You warned us. We won't be scared'**).

14 'When you see the disgusting thing that brings destruction set up where it ought not to be (**the person reading this needs to work out what I mean!**) then those in Judea should run as fast as they can

to the hills (**everyone pretends to run in place and shouts, 'Don't get caught in the valleys!'**) [15] The person on the rooftop shouldn't go down or go in and get anything from the house (**everyone shakes head and shouts, 'Don't go down!'**) [16] And the person in the field shouldn't go back to get a coat (**everyone shakes head and shouts, 'Don't go back!'**) [17] It will be awful for those who are pregnant or breastfeeding on that day (**everyone shakes head and shouts, 'Don't bring children into this!'**) [18] Pray that it doesn't happen in winter (**everyone shakes head and shouts, 'Don't get caught out in the cold!'**) [19] Those will be troubled days, the like of which have never happened from the start of creation – which God created – until now. Nor will there ever be the like again. [20] Unless God shortened those days, no human would survive; for the sake of his chosen ones whom he chose, he shortened the days. [21] If anyone says to you: "Look, there's the Christ," or "Look, he's there," don't believe them (**everyone says, 'You warned us. We won't be fooled'**). [22] False Christs and false prophets will be raised up and they will give signs and wonders so that, if they can, they will mislead the chosen ones. [23] But be careful, I've warned you about everything in advance (**again, 'You warned us. We won't be fooled'**).

[24] 'But in those days after the trouble, the sun will be darkened and the moon won't give it light (**everyone looks up and says,**

'Whoah!') ²⁵ And the stars will be falling from heaven and the powers in heaven will be shaken (**everyone keeps looking up, then tracks the course of the falling stars with fingers and goes 'Whoah!' again**). ²⁶ Then they will see the Son of Man coming on the clouds with huge power and glory (**one more big 'Whoah!'**) ²⁷ And then he will send angels and gather his chosen ones from the four winds, from the furthest point of earth to the furthest point of heaven (**everyone makes a big gathering-up motion with their arms**). ²⁸ Learn from the story of the fig tree: when its branch is already soft and it starts growing leaves, you know that summer is on the way. ²⁹ In the same way when you see these things happening, you know that he is near, he's at the door' (**everyone says, 'You have warned us. We will be ready'**).

Keep watch

³⁰ 'Listen carefully (**everyone puts a hand to an ear**) when I say to you that this generation won't pass away until all these things have happened (**everyone waves hand in front of body and goes 'Whoosh!'**). ³¹ Heaven and earth will pass away (**'Whoosh!' again**) but my words won't pass away. ³² But no one knows anything about the day or the hour when it will happen (**everyone looks at pretend watch on wrist and shrugs**) – not even the angels in heaven or the Son of Man (**more looking, more shrugging**) – only the Father

knows (**everyone looks at watch again, then looks up and gives a thumbs up**). [33] Be careful, keep watch (**everyone points to pretend watch!**) because you don't know when the moment will be. [34] It is just like a man leaving his house for a journey (**everyone waves and shouts, 'See ya later!'**) and putting his slaves in charge (**everyone waves and shouts, 'You're in charge, now!'**); each has a job to do and the doorkeeper is told to keep watch (**everyone shields eyes or creates binoculars in front of their eyes with their hands**). [35] Keep on watching then, because you don't know when the master of the house is coming; it might be in the evening (**everyone yawns**), it might be at midnight (**everyone hoots like an owl**), at the crack of dawn (**everyone rubs their eyes**) or in the morning (**everyone goes 'Cock-a-doodle-do!'**) [36] Otherwise he might arrive suddenly and find you napping (**everyone pretends to be asleep, little snore**). [37] What I say to you I say to everyone – keep watch!' (**Everyone wakes with a start!**)

Mark 14

A plot . . .

¹ Now the feast of Passover and Unleavened Bread was two days away and the chief priests and the scribes were looking for a way to grab hold of Jesus by trickery and kill him (**everyone whispers in a conspiratorial fashion to their neighbour, 'Let's grab him! Let's kill him!'**) ² For they kept on saying, 'Not during the feast because it might make the people riot.' (**Continuing in that conspiratorial mood, everyone says, 'But not during the feast. We don't want a riot!'**)

. . . and a grand gesture

(**Divide your group into two – one half for the woman, the other for the grumblers/Judas.**)

³ Jesus was in Bethany at the home of Simon the leper; he was stretched out at the dinner table when a woman came in. She had a jar of very expensive real perfume – called nard. (**The Woman group pretends to carry a jar. They carry it carefully, for what is**

inside is expensive.) She broke the whole jar and poured it on his head (**the Woman group pretends to break the jar and pour the contents lovingly on a pretend head**). ⁴ There were some people there who were outraged (**the Grumbler group cries, 'We're outraged!'**), asking why the perfume was wasted (**the Grumbler group cries, 'Why was this perfume wasted?'**): ⁵ 'This perfume could have been sold for over three hundred denarii and given to the poor.' (**The Grumbler group argues, 'Could have been sold for a shedload of money and given to the poor!'**) They grumbled at her (**the Grumbler group grumbles generally**). ⁶ But Jesus said: 'Leave her alone. Why are you causing trouble for her? She did a lovely thing for me (**the Woman group nods and says, 'I tried!'**) ⁷ You will always have the poor with you and whenever you like you can do good things for them, but you won't always have me (**the Woman group nods and says, 'That's right!'**) ⁸ She acted with what she had (**the Woman group nods and says, 'I did!'**); she anointed my body, preparing it for burial, in advance. ⁹ Listen carefully when I tell you that, wherever the good news is told throughout the whole world, what she did will be spoken in memory of her.' (**The Woman group says, 'That's amazing!'**) (¹⁰ Judas Iscariot, one of the Twelve, went off to the chief priests to hand Jesus over to them (**the Grumbler group says, 'I've had enough of this. I'm handing Jesus over to the chief priests'**). ¹¹ They were very pleased when they heard this and they promised to give him money (**the Grumbler group rubs hands together and says, 'And I'll make a little profit for my troubles!'**) So Judas started to look for easy ways to hand him over.)

The Passover meal

(**Everyone plays the disciples in this section.**)

12 On the first day of Unleavened Bread, when the Passover lamb was being killed, Jesus' disciples said to him (**everyone repeats the following line after you**): 'Where do you want us to go to prepare for you to eat the Passover?' 13 He sent two of his disciples and said to them: 'Go into the city (**everyone puts a finger on a finger, as if they are ticking off items on a list, and repeats, 'Go into the city'**) and a man will meet you (**a second finger, then say, 'A man will meet us'**), carrying a jar of water (**third finger and say, 'Carrying a jar of water'**). Follow him (**a fourth finger and say, 'Follow him'**) and, 14 wherever he goes (**a fifth finger and say, 'Wherever he goes'**), say to the person who lives in that house that "The teacher says, 'Where is the guest room for me to eat the Passover with my disciples?'" (**a sixth finger and say, 'Find the guest room.'**) 15 He himself will show you a large upstairs room furnished ready (**a seventh finger and say, 'He will show us the room'**). Prepare

there.' (**an eighth finger and say, 'Prepare there.'**) [16] The disciples went out, came into the city and found exactly what Jesus had told them – and they prepared the Passover. (**Everyone then holds up their hands, wiggling all their fingers, and all shout together, 'We did it!'**)

[17] When it was evening, Jesus came with the Twelve. [18] They were stretching out at the table and eating (**everyone makes eating motions and noises, carrying on through the following line**), when Jesus said: 'Listen carefully when I say to you that one of you who is eating with me will hand me over.' (**Now everyone suddenly stops eating and making noises.**) [19] They began to be really upset and said to him one by one: 'It isn't me, is it?' (**Everyone says in an upset way, 'It isn't me, is it?' – all together if a large group, one by one if a smaller group.**) [20] Jesus said to them: 'It's one of the Twelve – the one who is dipping with me into this dish. [21] The Son of Man is going away – just as it was written about him – but it will be awful for the person by whom he is handed over. It would have been far better for him if he had never been born.' (**Everyone sighs and shakes their head and says, 'Never been born . . .'.**)

[22] While they were eating, he took some bread, blessed it and broke it, and gave it to them and said: 'Take this, it's my body.' (**Everyone**

pretends to take a piece of bread, put it in their mouth and gently chew it.) [23] He took a cup and gave thanks and gave it to them and they all drank from it (**everyone pretends to take a cup and drink a little from it**). [24] And he said to them: 'This is my blood of the covenant which is being poured out for many people. [25] Listen carefully when I say to you that I won't drink (**repeat drinking motion**) what vines make again until I drink it fresh in God's kingdom.' (**Repeat drinking motion.**)

Jesus grieved and prayed . . . and the disciples slept . . .

[26] They sang a hymn and went out to the Mount of Olives. [27] Jesus said to them: 'You're all going to trip up in faith because it is written, "I will smash the shepherd and the sheep will scatter all over the place," [28] but after I've been raised I will go ahead of you to Galilee.'

[29] But Peter said to him: 'Even if they trip up in their faith, I won't.' (**Everyone repeats Peter's line, in a forceful manner.**) [30] Jesus said: 'Listen to me carefully when I tell you that this very night, before a cock crows twice, you will say you don't know who I am three times.' [31] But Peter said forcefully: 'Even if I've got to die with you, I'll never, ever deny you.' (**Everyone repeats Peter's line, even more forcefully!**) They all said the same. (**Everyone shouts, 'And the rest**

of us, too!') ³² They came to a place called Gethsemane and Jesus said to his disciples, 'Sit here while I pray.' ³³ He took Peter, James and John with him. He started to get upset and really distressed. ³⁴ Jesus said to them: 'My soul is incredibly sad, so sad I feel like death – stay here and keep watch for me.' (**Everyone shields eyes as if looking out.**) ³⁵ He went a little way away and fell on the ground and started to pray that if it were possible the hour might pass him by. ³⁶ He said: 'Abba, Father, everything is possible for you; take this cup away from me; but not what I want, what you want.' ³⁷ He came back and found them asleep (**everyone lays head on hands and snores**) and he said to Peter: 'Are you asleep? Haven't you got what it takes to stay awake even one hour? ³⁸ Keep watching and praying that testing times don't come your way – the spirit is keen but the flesh is feeble.' ³⁹ He went away again and prayed, using the same words. ⁴⁰ He came back and found them asleep again (**everyone repeats sleeping motion**) – their eyes were really heavy; they had no idea what to say to him (**everyone yawns and rubs eyes**). ⁴¹ He came a third time and said to them: 'Are you still asleep? (**Everyone repeats sleeping motion.**) Having a rest? The hour has come – look, the Son of Man is being handed over into the hands of people who do the wrong thing. ⁴² Get up, we need to go (**everyone stands up**). Look, the person who is going to hand me over is near.'

. . . and then ran away

(In this section, everyone plays the people who have come to arrest Jesus.)

[43] Right away, while Jesus was still speaking, Judas (one of the Twelve) arrived. There was a crowd with him from the chief priests, the scribes and the elders. They had swords and wooden clubs (**everyone pretends to wave swords and clubs and makes threatening sounds**). [44] Judas, the person who was about to hand him over, had given the crowd a sign, saying: 'The person I kiss is the one. Grab him and take him away securely.' (**Everyone repeats Judas's lines.**) [45] He came and, right away, said to him, 'Rabbi,' and kissed him gently (**everyone says, 'Rabbi,' and makes a gentle kissing sound**). [46] They laid hands on him and grabbed him. [47] But one of those standing there drew a sword and hit the slave of the high priest. He cut off his ear (**everyone grabs their ear and shouts, 'Owww!'**) [48] Jesus answered and said: 'Do you have to come out to snatch me with swords and wooden clubs, as though I'm a robber? (**Everyone repeats sword- and club-waving motion.**) [49] I was with you every day in the Temple, when I was teaching, and you didn't grab me then. But this is so that the Scriptures can be fulfilled.'

[50] They left him and ran away as fast as they could. [51] A young man was following along with him. He was wearing a linen sheet

but nothing else. They grabbed him (**everyone pretends to grab someone and cries, 'Gotcha!'**) [52] But he left the linen sheet behind and ran away naked (**everyone looks at empty hands and shouts, 'Rats! He got away!'**)

Jesus on trial . . .

(**In this section, everyone plays the people who are against Jesus, both officials and witnesses.**)

[53] They took Jesus to the high priest and all the chief priests and elders and scribes gathered together (**everyone raises their fist and makes angry, threatening sounds**). [54] Peter followed him (though not too close) right into the high priest's courtyard. He sat with the servants and warmed himself with the fire.

[55] The chief priests and the whole council kept on looking for proof against Jesus so they could put him to death (**repeat threatening sounds**), but they couldn't find anything. [56] Many people told lies about him but what they said didn't match up. [57] Some stood up and told lies about him, saying: [58] 'We heard him saying, "I will destroy this Temple made with hands and after three days I'll build another one without hands"' (**everyone repeats this testimony**). [59] Even then what they said didn't match up. [60] The high priest stood

up in the middle of them all and asked Jesus: 'Have you got no answer at all? What are they saying about you?' (**Everyone stands and repeats the high priest's lines.**) [61] Jesus kept silent and gave no answer at all. Again the high priest asked him and said: 'Are you the Christ? The Son of the Blessed One?' (**Everyone repeats the high priest's lines.**) [62] Jesus said: 'I am, and you will see the Son of Man sitting at the right hand of power and coming on the clouds of heaven.' [63] The high priest ripped his clothes (**everyone pretends to tear clothes and cries out in anger**) and said, 'Why do we need any more witnesses? [64] You heard the terrible thing he said. What does it seem like to you?' They all condemned him and said he deserved to die (**everyone shouts, 'He deserves to die!'**) [65] Some began to spit at him (**everyone makes spitting sounds**). They blindfolded him and punched him, saying, 'Prophesy!' (**everyone makes a punching motion and shouts, 'Prophesy!'**) and then the servants took him and beat him up (**more punching motions**).

. . . and then Peter on trial

(**Divide your group into three. One third will play Peter, one third will play his accusers and one third will play the rooster.**)

[66] Peter was downstairs in the courtyard; one of the high priest's servant girls came. [67] She saw Peter warming himself (**the Peter**

group pretends to warm their hands in front of a fire), looked him up and down and said (the Accuser group looks closely at the Peter group, then repeats the following line): 'You were also with Jesus of Nazareth.' [68] Peter denied it and said (the Peter group shakes their head vigorously and repeats the following line): 'I don't know or have any idea what you are talking about.' And he went out to the gateway. A cock crowed (the Rooster group crows). [69] The servant girl saw him and started saying again to the people standing around (the Accuser group points to the Peter group and repeats the following line): 'This man *is* one of them.' [70] He denied it again (the Peter group shakes their head even harder and shouts, 'No!') After a bit the people standing around said to Peter (the Accuser group repeats the following lines, firmly): 'You have to be one of them – you're from Galilee.' [71] Peter began cursing and swearing (the Peter group stands up, stomps around and shouts the following lines): 'I don't know the man you're talking about.' [72] Right away a cock crowed for the second time (the Rooster group crows). Then Peter remembered what Jesus had said to him: 'Before a cock crows twice, you will deny me three times.' Peter fell down and sobbed. (Those in the Peter group collapse into their seats, bow their heads and hide their faces in their hands.)

Mark 15

Jesus on trial before Pilate

(Divide your group into two – one half to play Pilate, the other to play the chief priests, elders, scribes and members of the council and the crowd.)

[1] Really early the next morning, the chief priests got together with the elders, the scribes and the whole council for a meeting **(the CP group looks at each other and mumbles together, as if scheming)**. They bound Jesus' hands, took him and handed him over to Pilate. [2] Pilate asked him **(the Pilate group points their finger and repeats the following line)**: 'Are you the King of the Jews?' Jesus answered: 'You are saying so.' [3] The chief priests began to accuse him of a lot of things **(the CP group points and mutters angrily)**. [4] But Pilate asked him again **(the Pilate group holds out their hands and repeats the following lines)**: 'Aren't you going to say anything? Look how many things they are accusing you of!' [5] But Jesus didn't give any other answers at all, so that Pilate was surprised.

⁶ At the feast he used to let a prisoner go – one that they asked for. ⁷ There was someone called Barabbas who had been put in prison with the rebels who had committed murder in the rebellion. ⁸ The crowd went up and started asking Pilate to do what he usually did **(the CP group shouts, 'Let one of your prisoners go!')** ⁹ Pilate asked them **(the Pilate group holds out their hands again and repeats the following question)**: 'Do you want me to let the King of the Jews go for you?' ¹⁰ (He knew that the chief priests had handed Jesus over because they were jealous of him.) ¹¹ But the chief priests stirred up the crowd to ask him to let Barabbas go instead **(the CP group shouts, 'No, let Barabbas go!')** ¹² Pilate said to them again **(the Pilate group repeats the following question)**: 'So what do you want me to do with the King of the Jews?' ¹³ They shouted back: 'Crucify him!' **(The CP group shouts, 'Crucify him!')** ¹⁴ Pilate kept on saying to them **(the Pilate group holds out their hands and repeats the following line)**: 'Why, what bad thing has he done?' But they shouted even louder: 'Crucify him!' **(The CP group shouts, 'Crucify him!' over and over again.)** ¹⁵ Pilate wanted to please the crowd, so he let Barabbas go and handed Jesus over to be beaten with whips and then crucified.

Mocked and beaten by the soldiers . . .

¹⁶ The soldiers led him away into the palace, which is the Roman governor's official residence, and called together the whole Roman

cohort (**everyone sighs and says, 'That's hundreds of soldiers'**).
¹⁷ They dressed Jesus in purple cloth and put on him a plaited crown made of thorns. ¹⁸ And they began to salute him: 'Hail, King of the Jews!' (**Everyone sighs and says, 'A mock coronation. Just to humiliate him!'**) ¹⁹ They kept beating his head with sticks, they spat on him and fell to their knees and worshipped him. (**Everyone puts their hands in front of their eyes and sighs, 'It's too awful. We can't look.'**) ²⁰ And when they had made fun of him, they took off the purple cloth and put his own clothes back on and they led him out to crucify him. (**Everyone sighs and says, 'There's no escape now.'**) ²¹ They forced a passerby – someone called Simon from Cyrene who was coming in from the country (the father of Alexander and Rufus) – to take his cross. ²² And they brought Jesus to the place called Golgotha, which if you translate it means 'the place of the skull'. ²³ They gave him wine mixed with myrrh (to make him sleepy) but he didn't take it. (**Everyone asks, 'Why not?'**) ²⁴ They crucified him and divided his clothing, throwing small pebbles to decide who had what. (**Everyone says, 'How callous!'**) ²⁵ It was the third hour (nine o'clock in the morning) when they crucified him.

. . . and then crucified

²⁶ The written charge against him read: 'The King of the Jews'. (**Everyone shakes their head and says, 'Mocking.'**) ²⁷ They crucified

him with two robbers, one on his right and the other on his left. [29] The people who passed by said terrible things about him, shaking their heads and saying: 'Huh, so this is the one who will destroy the Temple and rebuild it in three days. [30] Save yourself and come down from the cross.' (**Everyone sighs again and says, 'More mocking.'**) [31] In the same kind of way the chief priests made fun of him among themselves, along with the scribes; they said: 'He saved others, but he can't save himself. [32] The Messiah, the King of Israel, needs to come down from the cross, then we will see and believe!' (**Everyone sighs and says, 'And even more mocking.'**) Those being crucified with him also had a go at him.

[33] When the sixth hour came (twelve o'clock), it became dark over the whole earth and it lasted for three hours. (**Everyone whispers, 'It's dark.'**) [34] And at the ninth hour (three o'clock) Jesus cried out in a loud voice: 'Eloi, eloi, lema sabachthani!' which if you translate it means, 'My God, my God, why have you forsaken me?' (**Everyone whispers, 'He's calling.'**) [35] And some of the people standing around heard him and said: 'Look, he's calling for Elijah.' [36] Someone ran and filled a sponge with wine vinegar and put it on a long stick and gave him a drink (**everyone whispers, 'He's thirsty'**), saying: 'Let's see if Elijah comes to take him down.' [37] Jesus gave a loud cry and took his last breath. (**Everyone whispers, 'It's finished.'**)

³⁸ The curtain in the Temple was ripped in two from the top to the very bottom. (**Everyone says, 'See, it's ripped!'**) ³⁹ When the centurion who was standing right in front of him saw that he had taken his last breath, he said: 'This man really was God's Son.' (**Everyone says, 'See, it's obvious!'**) ⁴⁰ There were some women looking on from a distance; among them were Mary from Magdala, Mary the mother of little James and Joses, and Salome. ⁴¹ When Jesus was in Galilee they used to follow him and take care of him, and there were many other women who had come up with him to Jerusalem. (**Everyone says, 'See how much he was loved!'**)

Then he was buried

⁴² Evening came. It was preparation day, the day before the Sabbath.
⁴³ Joseph from Arimathea came. He was an important member of the council and was waiting for the kingdom of God. He dared to go to Pilate and asked for Jesus' body (**everyone holds out their arms as if asking for something**). ⁴⁴ Pilate was surprised that Jesus had died already (**everyone looks shocked**), so he called the centurion and asked whether he had been dead for a while. ⁴⁵ When he had the facts from the centurion he let Joseph have Jesus' dead body (**everyone holds out their arms as if handing something over**).
⁴⁶ Joseph bought a fine linen cloth, took Jesus down, wrapped him in the fine linen (**everyone makes a wrapping-up motion**) and put

him in a tomb, which was carved out of rock. He rolled a stone over the door of the tomb **(everyone pretends to push the stone to close the entrance to the tomb).** [47] Mary from Magdala and Mary the mother of Joses looked on to see where they had put him **(everyone makes a hand-over-eyes watching motion).**

Mark 16

Sunday morning

[1] When the Sabbath was over, Mary from Magdala, Mary the mother of James, and Salome bought spices so they could go and anoint Jesus (**everyone pretends to hold spices carefully in cupped hands**). [2] Really early on the first day of the week (**everyone yawns**), they came to the tomb just as the sun had risen. [3] They kept on saying to each other: 'Who will roll away the stone in front of the tomb for us?' (**Everyone shrugs as if asking the question.**) [4] They looked up and saw that the stone – which was really big – had already been rolled away! (**Everyone looks shocked!**) [5] They went into the tomb and they saw a young man, sitting on the right wearing bright white clothes, and they were really frightened (**everyone trembles with fear**). [6] He said to them: 'Don't be frightened; the Jesus you are looking for – the one from Nazareth who was crucified – he has risen. He isn't here. Look, this is the place where they put him. (**Everyone pretends to have a look at that place.**)

[7] 'Go, tell his disciples (including Peter) that he is going before you to Galilee. You will see him there just like he told you.' [8] The women went out from the tomb and ran away. (**Everyone runs in place.**) They were shaking and terrified and said nothing to anyone because they were so afraid. (**Everyone trembles again!**)